A TRAVEL GUIDE TO

Shakespeare's
London

A TRAVEL GUIDE TO

Shakespeare's
London

Other books in the A Travel Guide To series:

Ancient Alexandria
Ancient Athens
Ancient Rome
California Gold Country
Renaissance Florence

Shakespeare's
London

James Barter

**LUCENT
BOOKS®**

THOMSON
GALE

San Diego • Detroit • New York • San Francisco • Cleveland • New Haven, Conn. • Waterville, Maine • London • Munich

LIBRARY OF CONGRESS CATALOGING-IN-PUBLICATION DATA

Barter, James, 1946–
    Shakespeare's London / by James Barter.
        p. cm. — (A Travel Guide To:)
    Summmary: A visitor's guide to London in 1604, including what to see, where to stay,
    and where to eat, with sidebars on such topics as proper etiquette, famous residents,
    and student life at Oxford.
    Includes bibliographical references (p.) and index.
        ISBN 1-59018-146-8 (hardback : alk. paper)
        1. London (England)—History—16th century—Juvenile literature. 2. Shakespeare,
    William, 1564–1616—Homes and haunts—England—London—Juvenile literature. 3.
    London (England)—Social life and customs—16th century—Juvenile literature. [1.
    London (England)—Social life and customs—17th century.] I, Title. II. Series.
        DA680.B37 2003
        942.105—dc21

                                                                          2002003286

Printed in the United States of America

Contents

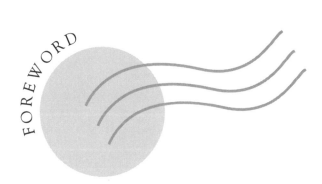

Travel can be a unique way to learn about oneself and other cultures. The esteemed American writer and historian, John Hope Franklin, poetically expressed his conviction in the value of travel by urging, "We must go beyond textbooks, go out into the bypaths and untrodden depths of the wilderness and travel and explore and tell the world the glories of our journey." The message communicated by this eloquent entreaty is clear: The value of travel is to temper one's imagination about a place and its people with reality, and instead of thinking how things may be, to be able to experience them as they really are.

Franklin's voice is not alone in his summons for students to "travel and explore." He is joined by a stentorian chorus of thinkers that includes former president John F. Kennedy, who established the Peace Corps to facilitate cross-cultural understandings between Americans and citizens of other lands. Ideas about the benefits of travel do not spring only from contemporary times. The ancient Greek historian Herodotus journeyed to foreign lands for the purpose of immersing himself

in unfamiliar cultural traditions. In this way, he believed, he might gain a firsthand understanding of people and ways of life in other places.

The joys, insights, and satisfaction that travelers derive from their journeys are not limited to cultural understanding. Travel has the added value of enhancing the traveler's inner self by expanding his or her range of experiences. Writer Paul Tournier concurs that, "The real meaning of travel, like that of a conversation by the fireside, is the discovery of oneself through contact with other people."

The Lucent Books' Travel Guide series enlivens history by introducing a new and innovative style and format. Each volume in the series presents the history of a preeminent historical travel destination written in the casual style and format of a travel guide. Whether providing a tour of fifth-century B.C. Athens, Renaissance Florence, or Shakespeare's London, each book describes a city or area at its cultural peak and orients readers to only those places and activities that are known to have existed at that time.

A high level of authenticity is achieved in the Travel Guide series. Each book is written in the present tense and addresses the reader as a prospective foreign traveler. The sense of authenticity is further achieved, whenever possible, by the inclusion of descriptive quotations by contemporary writers who knew the place; information on fascinating historical sites; and travel tips meant to explain unusual cultural idiosyncrasies that give depth and texture to all great cultural centers. Even shopping details, such as where to buy an ermine, trimmed gown or a much-needed house slave, are included to inform readers of what items were sought after throughout history.

Looked at collectively, this series presents an appealing presentation of many of the cultural and social highlights of Western civilization. The collection also provides a framework for discussion about the larger historical currents that dominated not only each travel destination but countries and entire continents as well. Each book is customized by the author to bring to the fore the most important and most interesting characteristics that define each title. High standards of scholarship are assured in the series by the generous peppering of relevant quotes and extensive bibliographies. These tools provide readers a scholastic standard for their own research as well as a guide to direct them to other books, periodicals, and websites that will provide them greater breadth and detail.

The Elizabethan Age

The year is 1604 and London is at the pinnacle of a glittering renaissance that began nearly fifty years ago with the coronation of Queen Elizabeth. The city is more beautiful than it has ever been and leads the entire nation as the commercial, social, and cultural center of England. Well-to-do ladies and gentlemen throughout England as well as other European nations have been flocking here to experience the finest that London has to offer in theater, art, architecture, stately aristocratic mansions, historic sites, and sumptuous foods. The city has never been a better destination for travelers.

Thanks largely to the efforts of the late queen who died last year, ending a forty-five-year reign, the citizens of London are enjoying what historians have been calling the greatest period in English history. A sense of cultural excitement runs throughout the city, because the good queen was an ardent supporter of English culture, particularly the arts. To encourage the nation's literati to write in the English language, she supported a move away from Latin, which had been the official language. Although many of the intelligentsia at Oxford and Cambridge Universities opposed her decision, the queen continued to voice her opinion yet still generously fund both universities. Her support led to a burgeoning of literature as London writers and poets such as John Donne, Edmund Spenser, Francis Bacon, and Sir Walter Raleigh were inspired to write in English.

Under Elizabeth, theatergoers also benefited, not just from her support of the English language but from her role in establishing new theaters as well. As a result, Londoners are now entertained by the best playwrights in Europe. During the early years of Queen

Elizabeth's reign Christopher Marlowe, Thomas Kyd, and Ben Jonson entertained London audiences with many classic plays. More recently, a young man by the name of William Shakespeare has written several plays that are popular with people from all social classes. If he continues with his craft, some believe that he might one day be judged one of England's best.

To further encourage tourism, London work crews have been busily cleaning and repairing several architectural treasures that are now more than five hundred years old. Five of these prized landmarks—the Tower of London, Westminster Abbey, Westminster Palace, London Bridge, and St. Paul's Cathedral—have been refurbished and await the arrival of vacationers' carriages.

Although Queen Elizabeth has been succeeded by King James, Londoners continue to celebrate the queen's achievements during her long and glorious reign. Sightseers to London will also appreciate all she did to clean and modernize the city. Many believe that London is now the safest and cleanest city in Europe. And whether guests choose to make their stay on the north or south bank of the city's Thames River, many fine inns and taverns are available.

So, come join us. All that London has to offer our European neighbors is just a one-day trip across the Channel from the coast of France. Once here, you will enjoy experiences not available in other European capitals. London's very own John Stow eulogized the city just five years ago, saying,

Queen Elizabeth I beautified and modernized London to make the city a popular destination for travelers.

11

A panoramic view of London, a city famous for its splendid architecture and vibrant cultural life.

"Among the noble cities of the world that Fame celebrates, the City of London of the Kingdom of the English, is the one seat that pours out its fame more widely, sends to further lands its wealth and trade, and lifts its head higher than the rest."[1]

CHAPTER ONE

A Brief History of London

Sightseers wandering the cobblestone streets of modern London will not find evidence of the city's origins. The major structures that dominate the city's central district cover any remnants of the earliest peoples who once inhabited this plot of land. Although the origins of the city date back more than two thousand years to 500 B.C., finding evidence beyond the improbable stories told by contemporary chroniclers is impossible. Most people today recognize that the region surrounding London was once inhabited by several self-governing tribes of relatively simple peoples, but unfortunately, none wrote histories. This has left many questions about their origins, cultures, and relationships with one another. It was not until much later that the first literate culture came here bearing Roman battle standards from across the Channel.

London Under the Romans

Far more information is known about London under Roman rule than under the earlier tribes. In 54 B.C., the great Roman general and statesman Julius Caesar passed through the present site of London on his way up the Thames River to subdue one of the many tribes living in the area.

Not until A.D. 43, however, did Roman history record the name of a small military outpost in the area called Londinium. Londinium had been established by the Romans after their invasion of England under the emperor Claudius. The Roman outpost began as a dirt and wooden walled military camp for soldiers, and included the first wooden bridge across the Thames River at the very place where the London Bridge now stands. At the time, the Roman camp only occupied the northern side of the river in the area that today is generally bounded by

Gracechurch Street and Fenchurch Street.

By the beginning of the third century, Londinium's population had exploded to an estimated fifteen thousand people, and by the year 350, the number had doubled. By this time, Londoners lived in a modern city. Londinium boasted a few paved streets, temples, public baths, offices, shops, bakeries, glassworks, modest homes, and a few elaborate villas for the Roman governor and wealthy merchants. The wall around the city was made of eight-foot-thick stone running three miles long and standing twenty feet high. The wall around London today follows this same route.

Roman general and statesman Julius Caesar (standing on the galley, right) lands his army on the coast of Britain and engages the enemy Celtic tribes.

The Roman Camp

The primary aims in establishing a fortified *castrum*, the Latin word for "camp," such as Londinium were twofold. The physical barrier was intended to enable the occupying Roman force to use it as a place of operations for subduing local opposition and to protect the legions in the event of an attack.

When planning a new town, Roman civil engineers used the same design and construction standards that they had used on previous camps. According to the design standards for military camps, the layout was always square or rectangular—Londinium was about eight blocks long and six wide—surrounded by high walls. Entry to the camp was through one of four gates located at the four points of the compass. Two main streets were laid out at right angles to each other, forming an intersection in the middle of the town. The road running north-south was always named *via principia*, main street, and the one running east-west was always named *via praetoria*, commander street. Both of these streets extended outside the town through the four fortified gates in the outer defensive wall. All secondary streets were also built straight and at right angles to each other.

Using this camp as a base of operations, the Roman soldiers subdued resistance to their expansion as they pushed north. As the importance of the camp grew, and the population increased with wives and children, large public buildings were added within the camp to provide for the needs of the Roman citizens. As camps expanded, as was the case with many Roman camps, large modern cities such as London eventually emerged.

During the course of the fourth and fifth centuries, Londinium fell into obscurity as the Roman Empire began to collapse and the legions protecting the city withdrew closer to Rome to protect the empire's capital. During that dark time, when regional warfare went unchecked by a national army, Germanic people called Saxons invaded England and replaced the Romans in Londinium.

London Under the Saxons and Normans

In the sixth century, the Saxons had firm control of Londinium and established it as a major trading center. Christianity was introduced to the city, but the inhabitants resisted and eventually drove the bishop away. Londinium was later sacked and burned by the Danes in the early ninth century, but was resettled by the Saxon king Alfred in 883, when the Danes were driven out. Alfred rebuilt the city walls and established a citizen army. English historians estimate the population to have been between ten and twelve thousand, considerably less than the population under the Romans.

Almost two hundred years later, Londinium began to develop districts that can still be seen today. The two centers of modern London, the monarchy and government building in the west end of the city at Westminster and the business sites in the east end, began during the reign of the last Saxon king, Edward the Confessor. He moved his residence two miles west of the city walls to be near the church he was building, Westminster Abbey.

In 1066, Edward the Confessor died without an heir to the throne. His brother-in-law, Harold II, was crowned king of England, although Duke William of Normandy, Edward's cousin, also staked

A portion of the Bayeux Tapestry depicts the death of Edward the Confessor. The tapestry is the most complete chronicle of the Norman invasion of England.

William the Conqueror's victory at the Battle of Hastings initiated Norman rule in England.

a claim to the English throne while living in Normandy, France. Later that year, William invaded England and drew up his army on the fields of Hastings on the east coast of England. Both armies collided on October 14. By the end of the day, Harold had been killed by an arrow shot through his eye and his army had been routed.

A few months later, William entered London and became the king of England. His coronation ended Saxon rule and initiated Norman rule, which would last for four centuries. At William's command, Londinium became known as Lunduntown.

King William I, known more commonly as William the Conqueror, was the first English monarch crowned at Westminster Abbey. Because he distrusted the remaining Saxon population in the city, William constructed a number of fortresses within the city walls, including the Tower of London and Westminster Palace.

Following William's death in 1087, a series of Norman kings ruled successfully.

They continued to build London's defenses as well as many of the cathedrals, royal palaces, and administrative offices that still stand high above the city. Over the next four hundred years, London became the commercial center of England and traded goods throughout Europe.

The city expanded dramatically, spilling beyond the walls east and west along the north bank of the Thames as well as across the river along the south bank. London's narrow streets became havens for shoppers, who visited thousands of small shops catering to the needs of the population. By 1300, London's population

The Normans constructed many buildings in London, including palaces like this one, which enhanced the city's visual appeal.

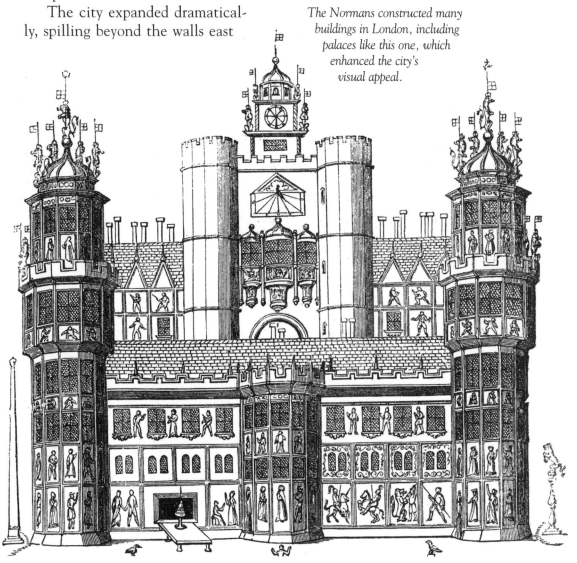

Tudor Architecture

In addition to constructing many great buildings in London, the five Tudor monarchs also added to and modified existing buildings over their more-than-one-hundred-year reign. One of the most interesting architectural features of homes and shops in London today comes from this period, and is named after the family, Tudor architecture.

Visitors walking the streets of London will see many examples of Tudor architecture, buildings that are framed with massive upright timbers often reinforced with diagonal members. The wooden beams, usually six inches on a side and stained black, are used to create a skeleton. The skeleton is then filled in with a mix of straw and plaster, locally called wattle and daub. The wattle and daub, which is long lasting but not strong, has no structural responsibilities; the wooden posts take the strain and the wattle and daub serves as decorative fill. The resulting construction is extremely durable as well as attractive.

Another unique characteristic of Tudor architecture sometimes seen in London is the use of imported brick. The use of brick is usually limited to decorative touches in homes and shops, such as on fireplaces, staircases, and arched entryways. Those with money, however, who wish to make a public statement about their wealth use brick instead of wattle and daub. The brick is typically set in a herringbone pattern that is beautiful outside and inside as well.

One of the great advantages of Tudor construction is the cost. Brick or wattle-and-daub buildings are cheaper to construct than stone buildings. Stone buildings involve immense labor, requiring the quarrying and transportation of heavy stone and specialized labor to set it properly.

Tudor construction also provides increased floor space. The Tudor style includes heavy beams on the second floor that cantilever four to six feet over the first floor. This engineering technique allows all of the upper floors to have more area than the first floor that supports the overhang.

had grown to thirty-five thousand, roughly half the population of Paris, the largest city in Europe.

The city suffered a devastating setback in 1348 and 1349 when the bubonic plague, commonly called the Black Death, struck London, killing two-thirds of its inhabitants. Nevertheless, the city rebounded and continued to prosper.

Between 1455 and 1485, a fierce civil war broke out that brought an end to Norman rule. Two of the most powerful families in England, Henry Tudor and the house of Lancaster, which had as its symbol a red rose, and the house of York, which had a white rose, clashed for control of the country. What ensued was the War of the Roses, so named because of the two families' symbols. In the end, at the Battle of Bosworth in 1485, Henry Tudor emerged victorious, becoming the first Tudor king and taking the name King Henry VII.

London Under the Tudors

The Tudor dynasty, which consisted of three kings and two queens between 1485 and 1603, is principally known for religious conflict followed by great prosperity and expansion for London. During the reign of the first Tudor, Henry VII, the population of the city grew to an estimated fifty thousand. Henry built several palaces outside the city walls and made additions to Westminster Abbey. Trade throughout England and Europe flourished, and for the first time London became a popular city for tourism.

When Henry VII died and Henry VIII took the throne, the building boom continued. Henry VIII's reign produced more significant buildings than that of any other English monarch. He erected Bridewell Palace, St. James' Palace, and Nonsuch Palace in London. However, of all Henry's palaces, his favorite residence was the one just a few miles downriver in the beautiful region of Greenwich.

Although London continued to thrive and expand under Henry's rule, his reign led to religious conflict after he and

A bustling London street in the time of the Tudors.

his wife failed to produce a male heir to the throne. Frustrated, Henry blamed his first wife, Catherine of Aragon, for giving birth to a girl, and he decided to pursue Anne Boleyn, whom he preferred and wished to marry in hopes of having a son. But divorce in England was not permitted, and the pope in Rome refused to grant him a divorce from Catherine so that he could marry Anne. Soon after, however, Anne became pregnant, triggering an explosive situation between the king and the pope. Following much diplomatic maneuvering, the enraged king withdrew himself and all English subjects from the Catholic Church and founded the Church of England. Although the new Church of England was led by the archbishop of Canterbury, final authority rested with Henry.

As problematic as Henry's decision was, the situation for the king and all of London only worsened. Since he was no longer bound by the pope in Rome, Henry divorced and then exiled Catherine so he could marry Anne, who promptly gave birth to another girl. From that point forward, Henry's rule became a reign of terror throughout London's upper class. Furious about having another daughter, Henry beheaded Anne in the Tower of London, along with many loyal advisers who now opposed his tyranny. By the time Henry died in 1547 without a male heir, many loyal friends and two of Henry's six wives had died on the chopping block.

In spite of the pall that Henry VIII's personal antics placed over London, the break from the Catholic Church was a stroke of good fortune for the city. At the start of Henry VIII's reign, London was filled with splendid Catholic buildings, religious treasures of previous centuries, and enormous holdings of land, all of which belonged to the pope. After his break with the pope, however, Henry confiscated church property, forcing Catholic churches to adhere to the Church of England and sell off land and monasteries. The proceeds he received from the sales went toward new construction in London, some earmarked for royal palaces and some for the benefit of all Londoners. Today, England remains loyal to the Church of England.

Following Henry's death were three other monarchs: King Edward VI, Queen Mary, and the last of the Tudor family, Elizabeth, who died last year. Of the three, Elizabeth was the longest reigning, the most ardent promoter of London's cultural offerings, and the most beloved by the city's population. With her death, London buried the last of the Tudors.

Modern London

London in 1604 has just begun the reign of the Stuarts with the coronation of King James. With a population of 200,000, the city is now the third largest in Europe—behind Paris and Naples, Italy—and is able to meet the needs and interests of tourists visiting our growing city. London has grown far beyond the walls, and now many new communities called suburbs, from the Latin meaning "below the city," are springing up such as Westminster, Southwark, Kensington, and Charing Cross.

The tallest buildings in London, aside from cathedrals and palaces, are four to six stories, but many smaller ones top off at two or three. Because the city has so many small businesses, the first floor of most buildings is occupied by shops, with family lodging on the upper floors. And often, inns rent the upper floors to travelers.

Sightseers will notice a distinct architectural motif on many buildings that are constructed of large heavy vertical and horizontal wood beams, with an application in between of thick light-colored stucco. When the building is completed, the beams are painted black. These buildings have been labeled by some today as "Tudor" architecture, named after the previous ruling family.

Now is the best time ever to visit London. Several festivals celebrating the coronation of King James are scheduled, and there is enthusiasm throughout the city for another reign as successful as that of Elizabeth.

CHAPTER TWO

Weather and Location

The Weather

The character and tempo of activities in London change with the seasons. London winters are warmer than in northern England, yet cool and wet compared to southern cities such as Rome and Athens. However, travelers from as far north as Copenhagen, Edinburgh, and Stockholm will find the winter weather a welcome relief from ice, snowdrifts, and long days of winter darkness. During the winter months, the average temperature in London is 40 degrees Fahrenheit, with light rain and a handful of days with thick fog, referred to by Londoners as "pea soupers." Although temperatures below freezing are rare, the Thames River occasionally freezes for short periods. In general, winter weather restricts most tourist activities to indoor entertainment such as shopping, viewing the city's great architectural masterpieces, and of course, attending the world-renowned theaters, all of which stay open during the winter.

Late December is an especially busy time in London—not so much because of Christmas celebrations but because many English pass through London on pilgrimages to Canterbury to commemorate the death of St. Thomas à Becket each December 29. Despite the crowds, foreign visitors will find plenty of inns and taverns to choose from and find better rates than during the warmer summer season.

Although there is much to be seen and bought inside London's hundreds of small shops year-round, it is not until spring that the city experiences a revival of its energy and beauty. Temperatures warm to a more appealing 62 degrees with clear, sunny skies, and rain tails off to about one inch a month. As the temperature improves, outdoor activities come to life, and the city's population swells with a tremendous influx of foreign visitors from Europe and Scandinavia.

By the time summer arrives, the temperatures warm to 70 degrees, with occasional bursts into the low 80s. The warmth spurs an open-air celebration of the many attractions that London has to offer. It is during the warm summer months that Londoners and their guests take to the streets and river to enjoy the many cultural activities and festivals. During the spring and summer, the citizens race to the streets to enjoy the open-air restaurants, food markets, curio shopping, sports events, boat rides on the Thames, festivals, theaters, and general sightseeing.

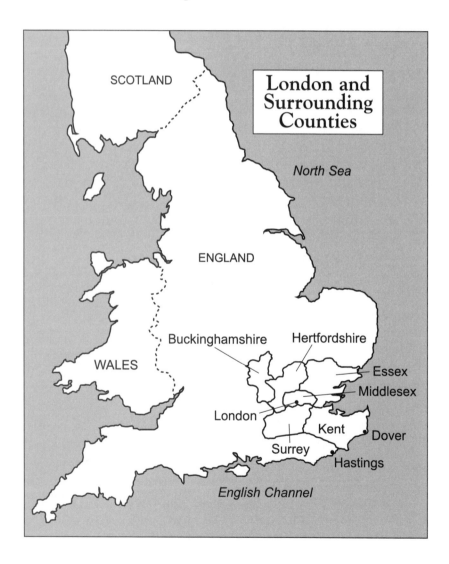

Location

Not every traveler is able to consult a map to locate London. Maps are a rare commodity, available to only the very rich and university scholars. For travelers without access to a map, London is located in the southeast corner of the island of Great Britain on the Thames River. The city is within Middlesex (meaning "Middle Saxon") County and is surrounded by the counties of Hertfordshire, Essex, Surrey, Kent, and Buckinghamshire. Middlesex is one of the smallest counties in England, measuring only about three hundred square miles. Were it not for the presence of London, Middlesex would be a little known county.

London's location is strategic. It originally served as a transportation center for trade goods, armies, messengers, and travelers in Roman England and continues in this same capacity today. London is situated just twenty miles up the Thames River from the Channel. Passengers arriving in London can easily board smaller boats and continue traveling farther upriver or take a carriage along any of the major roads connecting London with other cities. Although other English cities such as Dover and Hastings are actually closer to the French coast than London is, only London is located on a large river leading to the interior of the country.

London's position along the Thames is also a natural transition point for all foot and wagon traffic moving north and south. Unlike the relatively small Seine River in Paris, the Arno in Florence, or the Tiber in Rome, the Thames is a mighty river that cannot be easily crossed. Consequently, its 210-mile route across England creates a daunting watery obstacle for all north-south land travel. The only bridge over the Thames is the London Bridge, which is the only link for travelers, traders, and armies wishing to move north or south. In addition, because London experiences all traffic across the bridge, it becomes a natural stop along the route for rest and nourishment before moving on.

First Glimpses of London

The first view that visitors see as they approach London depends on their place of departure. For English citizens arriving from cities in the north, the first view of the city will be the spire of St. Paul's Cathedral, the tallest in all of Europe. Because London sits on a flat plain, travelers can see the spire from as far away as ten miles. The tall spire was intended as a landmark to guide visitors to the city. Upon arrival at the wall, weary travelers will have a choice of eight major gates through which to enter the city.

For travelers arriving by roads from the south, the first sighting will be the spire of St. Paul's and then the Thames River that splits the city in two. The city wall will not be visible

Travelers arriving in London by boat are treated to stunning views of the city. Bridewell Palace is on the right and London Bridge, in the distance.

because it protects only three sides of the city on the north bank, leaving the south side along the river exposed. The main road takes travelers through the heart of the entertainment section of the south bank district called Southwark. Travelers passing through this culturally rich and diverse district on Great Surrey Street will see on their left the cylindrical Globe and Rose Theatres, where plays are produced, and the Bear Garden and Bull Ring, where bears and bulls are baited by viscious packs of dogs. Finally, straight ahead, the Thames River will

appear, as will the south gate of the London Bridge, the only access to the north side of London.

European travelers arriving by boat from the Continent will enjoy the most dramatic entry to London as they first glimpse the city while sailing up the Thames. For these lucky adventurers, the first sights of the city will be the Tower on the right of the ship and then London Bridge straight ahead. Farther upriver to the right is St. Paul's spire, shortly followed to the left by the spire of Westminster Abbey. The ship will dock east of London Bridge, where all foreigners will pass through an inspection center called Custom House before being admitted to the city. London's popularity throughout Europe is reflected in Thomas Platter's observations of London docks when he arrived by boat in 1599:

Ocean craft are accustomed to run in here [London] in great number

The easily navigated Thames River helped establish London as one of the most important commercial centers of Europe.

as into a safe harbor, and I myself beheld one large galley next to another the whole city's length from St. Catherine's suburb to the bridge, some hundred vessels in all, nor did I ever behold so many large ships in one port in all my life.[2]

London's city walls have eight primary gates that are well fortified and guarded, as well as a series of postern,

or smaller, secondary gates. Travelers on foot can fit through the small narrow postern gates, but horses and carriages must pass through one of the eight primary gates. These gates have large arches, with the two largest being Moorgate and Aldgate.

The Thames River

London is a gift of the Thames. The river is wide and powerful, capable of floating the largest oceangoing vessels weighing as much as two hundred tons. Londoners recognized long ago that the river gave their city a marked commercial advantage over other significant English cities such as Birmingham, Northampton, Bristol, Hastings, and Salisbury. Of these major cities, only London provides traders and travelers with direct access to water transportation to commercial markets in Europe and to many English cities upriver toward the country's interior.

The Thames is everybody's thoroughfare. On London's behalf, the Thames makes possible the docks that supply London and the rest of England with European goods, as well as providing Europe with English goods. Here, dozens of ships tied to the wharves can be seen unloading exotic goods from all over Europe, the Middle East, and even a few from the New World. As goods are removed, buyers from England make their purchases and load their carts for the trip home. The smells of fresh fish, fruits and vegetables, and exotic spices on their way to London inns and taverns fill the air.

Of equal importance to Londoners, the river provides a line of defense against invaders from the south. To counter such a threat, the city built one bridge, and on it, architects designed two gates to protect the city should any insurgents attempt to storm across. The Thames also allows England's warships to patrol the city both east and west of London Bridge.

Besides providing for the city's transportation and defense, the river is also the great washer of all things. The sewage, dirt, and garbage that accumulate on London streets are washed down to the river during heavy rains. The Thames also washes Londoners who cannot afford the price of a bathhouse and cleans thousands of horses that are brought to the water to rid them of lice and road dirt. As if that were not enough, the Thames also accommodates the city's thriving beef industry by carrying away "butchers' pudding," the blood and entrails of slaughtered cattle, which eventually finds its way down the river and into the Channel. In addition, wool dyers, who must clean tons of wool used in the prosperous garment industry, wash it in the river.

The Thames is also a lovely place to visit. Cesar de Saussure, visiting from Spain, commented,

You cannot see anything more charming and delightful than this river. Above the bridge it is covered with craft of every sort; round about London there are at least 15,000 boats for the transport of persons and numbers of others for that of merchandise. Nothing is more charming and attractive than the Thames on a fine summer evening.[3]

Royalty have also displayed an appreciation of the Thames. During the reign of the Tudors, the Thames was in its greatest splendor. The monarchs of these times loved the river and lived in beautiful riverfront palaces at Hampton Court, Kew, Richmond, Whitehall, and Greenwich. The Thames provided an elegant setting for their royal barges, as Henry Machyn observed:

And after supper, the Queen's grace rowed up and down the Thames, and a hundred boats about her grace, with trumpets and drums and

English travelers wishing to visit London can take advantage of comfortable and efficient carriage services from convenient points of departure.

Coach Schedule to London

In 1597, John Taylor of London printed this schedule of various types of service to London from a variety of English cities. "Poste" refers to horses carrying mail, "foote-poste" means mail carried by a boy paid to run the mail, and "carrier" means a coach.

Prior to the printing of schedules, such as this one, the normal form was, to use the first entry of Bathe as an example, "The carriers of Bathe doe lodge at the Three Cups in Bred street, they do come on Wednesdaies and go away on Thursdaies."

Town	Means	London Inn	Days
Bathe	carrier	Three Cups, Bred Street	WTh
Buckingham	carrier	Kings Head, Old Change	WTh
Banbury	carrier	George neere Holborne Bridge	WThF
Cambridge	coach/waggon	Bull, Bishopsgate Street	ThF
Coventry	carrier	Axe, St Mary Axe or Aldermansbury	Th
Canterbury	foote-poste	Two necked Swanne at Sommerskey, Billsgt	WS
Hereford	carrier	Kings Head, Old Change	F
Ipswich	poste	Cross Keyes, Graceious Street	Th
Nottingham	carrier	Crosse Keyes, St John's Street	S twice daily
Nottingham	foote-poste	Swan, St John's Street	Th twice daily
Oxford	carrier	Saracen's Head without Newgate	near daily
Salisbury	carrier	Queenes Armes neere Holborne Bridge	Th

flutes and guns, and squibs [small sailboats] hurling on high to and fro, til 10 at night ere her grace departed and all the water-side stood with a thousand people looking on her grace.[4]

Traveling to London

The best way to get to London depends on each traveler's point of departure, pocketbook, and need for safety. Although London is a safe city once journeyers arrive, getting here must be carefully planned. Foreign travelers from the Continent must be willing to take their chances with high seas. English travelers, however, have several options.

Prior to departing for England from France, the Netherlands, Italy, Denmark, or Portugal, travelers should check the schedules of regular passenger routes on packet boats. Packet boats are sixty-ton sailing vessels that offer cabins on their high sterns. They have regular service direct to London from all major European cities. The voyage from Venice to London, for example, averages twenty-seven days; Copenhagen to London, nine days; and Lisbon to London, thirteen. Some packet boats offer luxurious services, including onboard dining, coal heaters, and night lamps. Once under way, the voyage is safe from pirates because the seas are kept open by the navies of all European countries. Foul weather, however, is always a risk, especially during the winter months.

If suffering through rough seas and seasickness for days is a painful thought, vacationers coming to London might consider horse and carriage travel to the French coastal town of Calais, just twenty-one miles across the Channel from Dover. Once at Calais, the trip across can be made in four hours if the currents and winds are favorable (it will take three times that in foul weather). In any case, the price is right, just five shillings. If your timing is right, merchant boats crossing the Channel will occasionally load passengers for just two shillings, but it is standing room only. Once in Dover, foreign travelers have the choice of purchasing a ticket for the seventy-mile coach ride to London or purchasing a ticket on one of the many barges that regularly make the short trip up the Thames.

English travelers wishing to vacation in London have more options than foreign vacationers. They can travel by land, by boat, or by a combination of the two. For persons of modest means, the cheapest way to travel to London is by foot or on one's own horse. Travelers who depart on foot can expect to cover twelve miles a day, while those on horseback can travel twenty to thirty. The major drawback to foot travel is the possibility of robbery; highwaymen occasionally accost travelers for their money and pickpockets sometimes cut the bottom out of a person's purse to get their coins. To thwart thieves, travel in large groups, wear the old shabby clothes of common workmen, and sew gold coins into the linings of heavy coats or cloaks.

For vacationers of means and in a hurry, renting horses, or traveling by post is an excellent alternative to using one's own horse. Post-houses are located at ten-mile intervals along all major roads leading to London. Each post-house is managed by a postmaster who cares for the horses, arranges for their availability, and provides rooms and

Proper Greetings

London society is primarily determined by one's social class. Class distinctions can be viewed everywhere by a person's dress, sword, horse, place of residence, and even his or her accent. Because maintaining class distinctions is so important, visitors to London will enjoy their stay more fully by learning how to greet Londoners properly in accordance with their social position.

If you do not belong to a noble family, either in England or in France, the first form of greeting is a quick but noticeable bow from the gentlemen and a curtsy from the ladies. Following that, address those above your rank as *"your worship," "your honor," "your lordship,"* or *"your ladyship."* If, however, in the highly unlikely chance that an invitation to meet King James is extended, he is addressed only as *"your grace."*

When meeting people of knightly rank, the following rules apply: When introduced to Sir John Packington, for example, he can be addressed as Sir John or Master Packington, but never as Sir Packington. Likewise, Captain Sir Francis Drake can be called Sir Francis or Master Drake or Captain Drake, but never Sir Drake. If an introduction is made to Sir Thomas Jermyn's wife Catherine, she can be called Catherine Lady Jermyn or Lady Jermyn, but not Lady Catherine.

When meeting people below knightly rank who are peers (barons and baronesses), these rules apply: If, for example, an introduction is made to Margaret Douglas, the countess of Lennox, she can be called Lady Lennox but not Lady Douglas. Sir William Cecil, Baron Burghley, the Lord Treasurer can be called Sir William or Lord Burghley or My Lord Treasurer, but certainly not Sir Cecil.

Following the greeting, any conversation should be brief. Only answer questions asked by royalty and never ask them questions. Conversations end when royalty take one step backward and utter any of these phrases: "How lovely," "That is very interesting," or "How nice." Never attempt a parting handshake unless a hand is offered first.

meals for weary travelers. Travelers who run their horses hard can expect to cover 100 to 150 miles a day. The disadvantage to this speedy travel is that it is expensive. Renters must hire post-boys to ride the horses back at the end of each leg of the journey. The cost of posting is three shillings a mile plus another four shillings for each post-boy to return the horse.

If greater comfort and safety is desired, sailing boats make regularly scheduled trips to London from major English cities such as Liverpool, Plymouth, Dover, Portsmouth, Gloucester, and Newcastle upon Tyne. Most of these boats carry commercial goods but are willing to find space for passengers.

Still another alternative for vacationers, and the favorite for most, is to purchase a ticket from one of the many private transport companies that provide carriages on regularly scheduled routes. Two of the best are the Brighton Carriage Company and the Shrewsbury Highflyer. Both maintain many fine inns along English roads where travelers can leisurely spend long hours at dinner before a cozy fire.

The Shrewsbury Highflyer leaves Shrewsbury at 8:00 each morning bound for London. The journey of forty miles proceeds in an unhurried manner. As an example of its leisurely pace, the first day it arrives at Chester at 8:00 in the evening, where dinner is offered at Wrexham Inn for as long as the passengers wish to eat. In summer, it stops at a local farmhouse renowned for the quality of its pork pies, allowing passengers to make purchases if they wish. The coach will even stop to let people make short visits to friends along the way.

However journeyers choose to arrive in London, hundreds of innkeepers, tavern owners, bankers, boat and carriage drivers, city guides, and dozens of other professionals are committed to making every visit as enjoyable as possible.

CHAPTER THREE

Arriving in London, Where to Stay, and Where to Eat

Arriving in London

Travelers arriving in London must enter through one of the eight gates along the city wall before 8:00 P.M. when the curfew bell rings, signaling guards to close and lock them. London's curfew dates back to the eleventh century when William the Conqueror implemented his *couvre-feu*, French for "cover the fire," or curfew. At the time, this meant that people had to extinguish all fires and candles at nightfall. The law was not originally intended to keep people off the streets but, rather, to prevent fires in the city at a time when building materials such as straw and thatched roofs were common. Over time, however, it has come to mean that everyone must be in their home.

The Night Watch, men who patrol the streets at night, stop and interrogate anyone wandering the streets after the curfew bell. Severe penalties are imposed on anyone caught disobeying the curfew without good cause. Fortunately for late arrivers, the curfew applies only within the city walls. Those arriving late will be able to find an inn for the night at any of the gates on London's west side outside the wall.

Compared to getting to London, getting around the city will be far simpler. However, before doing any traveling, it will be necessary to convert foreign currency into English money. Although many establishments will accept foreign money, the exchange rates are not favorable. Reputable currency exchanges can be found in banks and jewelry stores, where gold and silver coins are weighed and exchanged for the same weight in English coins. However, before exchanging coins, all first-time visitors need to understand England's unorthodox coinage.

English Money

English currency is very different from others throughout Europe and will be confusing for first-time visitors. When planning to arrive in London, bring only gold or silver coins, because for the past forty years English mints have only struck coins using those two metals and they will not accept coins made of brass, copper, or lead. Pay attention to the appearance of English coins because their values and names can be confusing.

The basic denominations are pounds, shillings, and pence. Twelve pence make

Visitors in London must heed the curfew bellman (pictured) to avoid an encounter with the Night Watch patrol.

a shilling, and twenty shillings make a pound. When prices are written, the following abbreviations are used: Penny is *d*, shilling is *s*, and pound is £. The English do not actually have a gold coin called the pound; instead, the coin that is worth one pound is called a sovereign. The sovereign is extremely rare. Londoners more typically carry a coin of lesser value called an angel, which is equivalent to ten shillings, and a half-angel worth five shillings. If you ever need to bribe someone in London, tell him that in exchange for what is needed, an angel will visit him.

The most commonly carried large coin is the crown worth five shillings, which is issued in both gold and silver.

London's Night Watch

Since the city does not have a municipal police force, Londoners are forced to rely on each other for protection against street crime. When night falls and Londoners go to bed at curfew, a different group takes to the streets to maintain law and order called the Night Watch.

The Night Watch is a group of primarily elderly men whose job is to patrol the streets of London watching for curfew violators, fires, and any other sort of disturbance. Crime continues to be a problem, and the night attracts some unsavory characters who engage in such criminal behavior as robbery, theft, prostitution, and witchcraft.

Each member of the Night Watch walks his assigned neighborhood carrying a lantern and a ten-foot-long pike to be used as a weapon. As members of the Night Watch make their rounds, they interrogate anyone on the street and make arrests if warranted. They also function as clocks, calling out the time each hour followed by the slogan "and all's well." Although some people resent being awakened by their calls, most fall back to sleep knowing that all is well in the neighborhood.

The Night Watch is paid a very small sum to patrol the streets of London. The fees for their services are raised in the neighborhoods they patrol. Shopkeepers are usually happy to pay for the protection their shops receive, and the general population also appreciates their fire calls and the ringing of the fire bell whenever necessary. Law-abiding citizens who cannot sleep often chat with members of the Night Watch during their patrol, and on occasion, when their duties for the night are over, they lend their lantern to help citizens start their morning fires for warming their homes.

The crown is roughly equal to a Venetian ducat, a Flemish gelder, or a French ecu. The half-crown is worth 2 shillings 6 pence, written 2s. 6d. The next smallest coin in value is the silver sixpence; then the silver fourpence, commonly called a groat; and the silver penny, called a penny, never called a pence. Below the penny is a half-penny pronounced ha'-penny and finally the farthing, which has the value of a quarter-penny.

Watch your money carefully. Although most Londoners are honest and respectable, a few are not. Pickpockets gravitate toward popular tourist attractions looking for distracted visitors.

Getting Around the City

London is divided into twenty-six wards, a city planning strategy that is beneficial to sightseers. Knowing the districts in which sights of interest are located will speed one's journey and help determine the most direct route when asking directions of Londoners. The twenty-six wards bear names such as Blackfriars, where St. Paul's Cathedral is located; the City of London, commonly referred to as simply the City, where the Tower and London Bridge can be found; and St. Katharines Dock, home of London's largest docks.

Walking the streets of London can be a pleasant way to see the city—as

The front and back of the English sovereign coin. Because such coins are uncommon, it is advisable to visit London with other currency.

long as the route is one that has been recently paved with cobblestone. These modernized streets are generally wide and are located in the most popular tourist areas. They are more reliable than unpaved streets because they are always open and they are cleaner. Pedestrians using the cobblestone streets will find that they arrive at their destination with clean and dry boots.

If one's journey is several miles, newly introduced carriages are now available for hire. Queen Elizabeth recently used a carriage and the idea caught on with several livery stables.

Carriages can be hired at several places throughout London. They are fast, dry, and best of all, four can ride for the same price as one. Although they lack springs to soften the ride, they are reasonably comfortable. Carriages are far more popular with London women than men. It seems that men feel carriages are for people who are old, ill, or physically weak. No self-respecting man would be found in one. Nonetheless, carriages can be hired for short trips or by the day at the bargain price of 8s. 6d.

A variety of boats are available for hire down by the river. Any of the

Many London streets are paved with cobblestone. This modern amenity allows tourists to arrive at their destinations with clean and dry boots.

wharves along the Thames have water ports where groups of watermen stand ready to taxi journeyers in small boats. For a short trip across the Thames, one can hire a small rowboat called a wherry, which provides passengers with upholstered cushions. The cost per person is one penny. For adventurers wishing to travel up or down the river, simply go to the wharf and holler out the direction of travel to the watermen with a loud shout of either "eastward ho" or "westward ho."

The price of a trip east or west is determined by the distance and tide. A trip from the Tower to Westminster Palace, for example, will cost 6 or 8d. depending on the direction of the tide. Rowing against the tide is harder work, it takes longer, and it costs more. Carefully timing a trip in either direction is prudent. Since London is not far inland from the English Channel, the direction of the river's current changes with the tide. Traveling with the tide rather than against it will make the trip faster and less expensive. A trip from central London to Westminster is 6d. with the tide, and a round trip to Chriswick is 2s. 6d. Besides the many wherries on the water, sightseers will be amazed by the number of sail-driven barges carrying cattle,

Cobblestone Streets

Travelers to London will appreciate the convenience of cobblestone. The need for cobblestone has been evident for years, but converting dirt and gravel streets to cobblestone is a slow and expensive undertaking.

Cobblestones, six-inch by six-inch cubes of rock neatly arranged in a bed of sand, take a long time to set. Workmen must first clear and smooth the dirt roads. They then crown the street, meaning they leave the middle of the street a few inches higher than the edges so that rainwater will drain to the sides and down the gutters. Workmen then apply several inches of sand to act as a firm cushion to keep the tops of the cobblestones level with one another so that carriage wheels will not bang against them and chip. After trimming each stone to fit, and using string guides to maintain alignment, workmen carefully set them into place in the sand, one stone at a time.

Cobblestones provide the greatest benefits during winter rains when muddy streets become impassable. However, they sometimes make carriages vibrate and bounce, causing passengers' teeth to chatter and their joints to ache. For pedestrians, the new cobblestone streets have an additional benefit: raised sidewalks. Constructed exclusively for people on foot, the sidewalks prevent horses and carriages from jostling walkers. London will soon have as many cobblestone streets as Paris.

wheat, coal, lumber, and boxes of fruit and vegetables from all over England.

If on your trip you pass under London Bridge, hang on tightly. When the tide is either exceptionally high or low, the level of water is higher on one side than on the other because the bridge obstructs its flow. Passing through the brief rapids is called "shooting the bridge" by the watermen, because the water can drop the boat four or five feet, giving the novice passenger a stomach-wrenching scare. There is a saying among some Londoners that wise men walk over London Bridge while only fools go under it.

Modern Conveniences

London's aldermen, the elected officials representing each of the city's twenty-six districts, have recently passed laws requiring that streets be lit at night. The laws require, among other things, that the owners of houses

Weary visitors may tour London by carriage. Here, a carriage awaits passengers in front of the Fortune Theater.

Clean and well-laid streets make a visit to London pleasurable, safe, and trouble-free.

or shops place a lantern and candle outside and keep it lit. This has greatly benefited people making their way in the evening. It has led to fewer injuries and has reduced petty crime, making the streets of London safer than ever.

The water system in London has also been modernized. Until recently, drinking water had been drawn from the Thames, but as the population increased, city officials and London's medical professionals recommended a cleaner water supply for the city. To meet the needs, a company called the New River Company was hired to pro-vide a system of pipes throughout London carrying freshwater from local springs north of the city walls.

The New River Company located several sources of freshwater and dug a forty-mile-long channel to bring the water into the city to several distribution points. At each distribution point, horses can drink and citizens can fill their water buckets. Families with moderate incomes hire water carriers, young boys, to deliver freshwater daily. In order to disperse the water more widely, underground pipes made of wood or lead carry the water into all districts of the city. Some of the larger buildings and homes can even pay to have the water piped directly into their residences. Although visitors to London can depend on the cleanliness of the water in the better inns and taverns, they may wish to drink only ales and fruit juices at the less expensive public establishments.

Vacationers will be especially pleased to know that London's streets, which in most parts have been nothing more than dirt in the summer and mud in the winter, are also being improved. The streets that lead to places of greatest interest to sightseers such as the Tower, Westminster Abbey, and St. Paul's Cathedral are now paved with cobblestone. Not only does this paving make for a better carriage ride, it also allows visitors to wear nice clothing and shoes without returning to their inns covered in mud.

Finally, as important to everyone as safe streets and good water, the city recently completed the Whittington Longhouse, a public privy on the Thames River at the south end of Friar Street and Greenwich Place. The privy is the largest in Europe, with two rows of sixty-four seats each, one row for men and the other for women. The seats overhang a gully, which is cleaned out by the daily tide that sweeps along the Thames. As visitors make their way around London, they will find the Longhouse to be a welcomed convenience.

Finding a Place to Stay

Once visitors have English coins weighing down their purse and know their way around town, it is time to find a good place to stay. Inns for travelers have been a part of London for the past four hundred years. London innkeepers are proud of their large selection of clean inns that will suit any traveler's budget. English traveler William Harrison talks about the high standards for cleanliness in London's inns in his book *The Description of England*:

Our inns are also very well furnished with napery, bedding, and tapestry. For besides the linen used at the tables, which is commonly washed daily, is such and so much as belongeth unto the estate and calling of the guest. Each comer is sure to lie in clean sheets . . . for every visitor may use the inn as his own house, so long as he logeth here. There is no greater security anywhere for travelers than in the guest inns of London.[5]

Travel through England has been a passion for the English for centuries. It has even been the subject of much great literature, such as Geoffrey Chaucer's late-fourteenth-century work *The Canterbury Tales*. Probably the most famous of all the inns is the Tabard, in Southwark, London, where Chaucer stayed before traveling to Canterbury.

The modern London travel writer Fynes Moryson, who writes stories about favorite vacation spots in Europe, describes the personal attention guests receive on their arrival at a London inn:

The world affords not such Inns as England hath, either for good and cheap entertainments at the guest's own pleasure, or for humble attendance on passengers. . . . For as soon as a passenger comes to an Inn the

Description of a London Inn

Londoner William Harrison published a wonderful book not long ago in 1587 called *The Description of England*, in which he provided this excellent description of London inns:

London has great and sumptuous innes builded in it, for the receiving of such travellers and strangers as passe to and fro. The manner of harbouring wherein, is not like that of some other countries, in which the host or goodman of the house dooth chalenge a lordlie authorities over his ghests, but cleane otherwise, with everie man may use his inne as his owne house in England, and have for his monie how great or how little varietie of vittels [foods], and what other service himselfe shall thinke expedient to call for. Our innes are also verie well furnished with naperie . . . bedding and tapisterie: for beside the linnen used at the tables, which is commonlice washed dailie, is such and so much as belongeth unto the estate and calling of the ghest. Ech commer is sure to lie in cleane sheets, wherein no man hath beene lodged since they came from the landresse. . . . If the traveller have an horsse, his bed dooth cost him nothing, but if he go on foot he is sure to paie a penie for the same: but whether he be horsseman or footman if his chamber be once appointed he may carie the kaie [room key] with him, as of his owne house so long as he lodgeth there. If he loose oughts whilest he abideth in the inne, the host is bound by a generall custome to restore the damage, so that there is no greater securitie anie where for travellers than in the gretest ins of England. Their horsses in like sort are walked, dressed, and looked unto by certeine hostelers or hired servants, appointed at the charges of the goodman of the house, who in hope of extraordinarie reward will deale verie diligentlie after outward appearance in this their function and calling.

servants run to him. . . . Another servant gives the passenger his private chamber and kindles his fire, the third pulls off his boots and makes them clean. The Host or Hostess visits him, and if he will eat with the Host, or at a common table with others, his meal will cost him sixpence, or in some places but fourpence. . . . If he have company especially, he shall be offered music, which he may freely take or refuse and if he be solitary, the Musicians will give him the good day with music in the morning.[6]

If vacationers prefer to arrive in London with their own horses and carriages, then a coaching inn is a more practical choice than a standard inn.

Lodging at a London inn typically includes a hearty meal at a festive dinner table.

Coaching Inns

Coaching inns are a vital part of the London coaching tradition. They differ from standard inns by offering food and lodging not only to travelers but to their horses as well. Besides caring for travelers and horses, the inns are part of a coaching system throughout England that rents carriages and other vehicles as well as the horses to pull them.

The coaching inns of London are larger than ordinary inns to accommodate horses and carriages. They are generally large buildings built around a central courtyard, where the horses are walked until they are cool and then they are washed and rubbed down before being fed.

One of the most highly regarded coaching inns of London is the Saracen's Head. The hostess, Mrs. Mountain, has a carriage builder's workshop on her premises to make any necessary repairs. She also maintains many coaches that are available for rent and keeps two thousand horses in her stables for the routes she serves. Mrs. Mountain claims that each horse costs her two pounds per week to feed, groom, and stall. The strains on a pair of horses pulling a carriage weighing more than two tons at an average speed of ten miles per hour is hard work. Mrs. Mountain estimates that the life of a coach horse is no more than three years. After that, she sells them as riding horses since they still have a long life.

Most coaching inns are located at the various gates surrounding London. Recommended coaching inns at Bishopsgate are the Bull, the Green Dragon, the Four Swans, and the Dolphin. At Aldgate, good coaching inns are the Three Nuns, the Blue Boar, and the Spread Eagle, and at Cripplegate, the Ram, the Bear and Ragged Staff, the King's Arms, the Black Swan, and the Horseshoe.

As arriving guests near a coaching inn, the driver or guard is advised to blow his horn to warn the innkeeper of their arrival. This will ensure that there is food on the table when the guests arrive and unpack. In addition to good clean places to sleep, many inns also offer meals. Although they are hearty and of adequate quality, current laws prevent innkeepers from charging more than sixpence per person. Consequently, vacationers looking forward to elegant dining will want to try one of London's hundreds of excellent taverns.

Finding a Good Tavern

Flavorful, hearty meals are more important to Englishmen than to Europeans living on the Continent, who prefer smaller but more artistically prepared meals. As one foreigner commented, "The English eat a great deal at dinner; they rest for a while, and do it again until they have quite stuff'd their paunch."[7] Breakfasts are usually skipped by most of London's working class, or at best consist of light leftovers from the previous day. The other two meals of the day, however, dinner served between 11:00 A.M. and noon and supper served between 6:00 and 9:00 at night, are both generous.

If gourmands prefer to try one of London's many fine taverns for dinner or supper instead of eating in their inns, there are hundreds to choose from depending on the size of their purses. One of the attractions of many taverns is their warm and cozy environment.

The nicer taverns create a leisurely atmosphere centered around a great blazing fireplace, an adjoining game-room for gambling and darts, flower arrangements filling the tavern with fragrance, rooms for pipe smokers, and comfortable leather chairs that make for great conversations. If such an environment sounds poetically elegant, it may be. Consider this poem extolling an inn's warmth and food written by William Harrison:

Elegant Dining

For those willing to spend as much as a half-crown for a truly memorable meal, the Robin Hood Tavern is the place to dine. Its sign is easily recognizable: Hanging above the entrance by a chain is a wood carving of Robin Hood in a green tunic and tights shooting his bow and arrow. The tavern is currently offering the following menu:

Venison Game Stew:
Venison meat, wine, lard, onion, pepper, oregano, toasted breadcrumbs, and vinegar.
Goat Kid Pie:
Goat kid meat, lard, aromatic herbs, saffron, soft cheese, and eggs.
Limonia:
Chicken breast, lard, onions, almonds, hard-boiled egg yolks, spices, and lemon juice.
Fritters with Elderberry Flowers:
Flour, ricotta cheese, salted cheese, yeast, eggs, milk, rose water, raisins, elderberry flowers, oil, butter or lard, and sugar.
Poached Sturgeon:
One whole sturgeon and white wine.
Rice with Almond Milk:
Almonds, goat's milk, rice, and sugar.

Continental travelers to London are often overwhelmed by the substantial portions of the tavern supper.

Good bread and good drink, a good fire in the hall,

Brawn [pig head], pudding and souse [ale], and good mustard withal.

Beef, mutton, and pork, sherd pies of the best,

Pig, veal, goose, and capon, and turkey well drest:

Cheese, apples, and nuts, jolly carol to hear,

As then, and is now, is counted good cheer.[8]

Near St. Paul's Cathedral are three favorite London spots where travelers come to satisfy their hunger. The fashionable Black Anchor, the Cheshire Cheese, and the Fox and Hound are three of the best taverns in this district. Londoners living here are often heard to comment that nothing has yet been thought of that brings more happiness than these taverns. Expect to pay between 1 and 2s. for a great meal, and remember to bring your own knife if you prefer to cut your meat rather than tearing it with your fingers and teeth. Although spoons will be provided at all taverns, forks are frowned on as being uncivilized and are better left at home.

Dinner or supper at any of London's better taverns will always begin with bread and softened butter, then an entremet, or appetizer, meant to prepare the stomach for the larger meal. The appetizer might be a seafood treat such as mussels, oysters, crab, or shrimp culled fresh from the English Channel. Also popular is the *soppet*, or leek poached in white wine and served on a piece of toasted bread. For the main course, any number of foods will be available once the trenchers are in place. For those new to London, trenchers are thick slices of stale bread used as plates to hold food. They will be periodically cleared away

Dining Etiquette

Understanding proper etiquette in public taverns will provide a comfortable evening for everyone. When dining at a tavern, remember that most food is eaten with the fingers. Although some people prefer to use knives, never use a fork. The food is always taken from the serving plate, then placed on the trencher, and then eaten. In addition to these regulations, the following rules are always observed in London:

Do not take food until the blessing is given, nor take a seat, except that which the master of the house chooses.

Never take up food with unclean hands.

Let your fingernails be trimmed.

Do not press the cheese and the butter onto your bread with your thumb.

When a piece of food has been touched by the teeth, do not put it back on the serving dish.

Do not scratch your limb, after the fashion of a mole, as you sit down or pick your nose.

Persons eating should not clean their teeth with their knife.

Do not spit over the table or down upon it ever.

If you can, do not belch at the table.

Never let a cat be a companion to you at the table.

Wipe your knife and wipe your spoon with your napkin.

Do not put your knife on your trenchers lest you be reproved.

Do not chew visibly on either side of the jaw.

and replaced with new ones during the course of the meal.

Among the favorite main dishes that connoisseurs can choose are roasted beef with pepper sauce, sliced breast of chicken in cinnamon sauce, baked mushroom pasties (a great pie made of venison, pork, and veal), baked trout in *sauce galyntyn*, boiled turnips with chestnuts, and sliced apples fried in ale batter. Dessert will generally include a selection of fresh fruits and French cheeses.

If the service has been exceptional, leaving the waitperson a *vail*, or tip, is always considered good form. Typically, leaving one or two pence is customary. Remember, a waitperson only makes between two and five pounds per year.

The Alehouse

If a glass of ale and a simple meal are more to your liking, visit any of London's alehouses. No other city offers a richer variety of alehouses than London. For those new to London and looking for a recommendation, ask for a good *tipping house*, the local term for alehouses. For French visitors, bear in mind that ale has a lower alcoholic content than wine, unless one orders double-strength ale called "double ale" or the more

A colorful London alehouse tradition involves the pewter drinking cup or tankard (pictured). Each patron is required to drink a measured amount of beer before passing the tankard to his neighbor.

expensive "double-double," which is also referred to by locals as "mad dog" or "dragon's milk."

Alehouses have a tawdry reputation as places where working-class men drink and eat simple foods, such as breads, meat cakes, chicken, and stew. They are particularly popular in poor districts of London because the water supply in those areas is often not clean, making ale the only safe drink. In addition, alehouses are also the cheapest place for a basic meal.

Gentlemen visiting London for the first time may find an evening in an alehouse to be a source of unusual excitement and entertainment. Excessive drinking often leads to colorful language, gambling, occasional fistfights, and visits by ladies, called Winchester geese, willing to entertain gentlemen for a price. Although most alehouses are policed by the owner or by a hired "bouncer," be advised to visit with friends and to hide your purses.

An old alehouse tradition that newcomers to London may find interesting is the pewter drinking cup, called a tankard, that is shared by many patrons. The tankard is measured on the outside by pegs. Each drinker is required to drink down to the next peg and then pass the tankard on. However, some drinkers often drink beyond the measure, taking the next drinker "down a peg or two," an expression often heard in alehouses.

For visitors vacationing on a tight budget, many alehouses provide rooms that are shared by several people. Guests are expected to share beds on bundles of straw spread on the floor. Blankets are provided, but the rooms typically have no windows, no heating, no furniture, and no security. Custom prevents women from spending the night in alehouses.

After a day of exchanging money, finding a good place to sleep, and eating a good meal, it is time to get a good night's rest before getting ready for the next day of visiting London's most famous and most important historical landmarks.

Historical Monuments of London

Londoners are proud of their city's architectural monuments. They are large, intriguing, and old, all dating back more than five hundred years to William the Conqueror or earlier. These monuments are stone statements about English history, English principles, and English character. First-time-to-London visitors will learn a great deal about this country's spirit by touring each of the four recommended sites in this chapter.

The first stop, moving east to west, will be the Tower of London, simply referred to as the Tower, one of the most interesting and infamous sites in the city. It is easy to locate because it anchors the southeast corner of the London wall at the river.

The Tower

The Tower remains one of London's most magnetic tourist attractions, as well as the most eerie. Famous through-out the world as one of the bloodiest sites in any capital city, the Tower is the prison and execution place of royalty, traitors, and common thieves. Sightseers arriving at the Tower today can walk around the wall; however, to enter, they must be invited by King James or be attending a public execution. Entrance to the Tower remains restricted and under the control of guards called the king's yeoman's warders, more common-ly known as the Beefeaters.

Although there have been many beheadings here, the history of the Tower encompasses more than bloody death. The Tower is actually a double-walled eighteen-acre compound, called a bailey, enclosing several large struc-tures. Its initial phase, built between 1066 and 1087 during the reign of William the Conqueror, included a keep, a walled palace from which guards could keep watch over the surrounding countryside, named the White Tower.

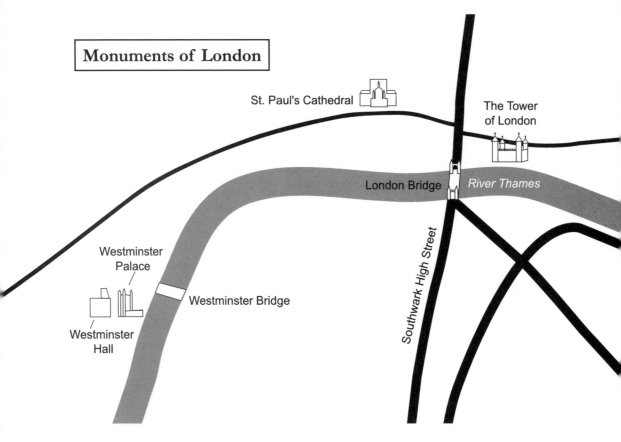

Monuments of London

St. Paul's Cathedral

The Tower of London

London Bridge

River Thames

Westminster Palace

Westminster Bridge

Westminster Hall

Southwark High Street

In addition to functioning as a keep, the White Tower was also William's palace. Initially built of wood, the ninety-one-foot-tall three-story White Tower today is stone. Such a fortification had never before existed in England, and all who saw it were said to have been terrified by its size and defenses. It was intended to protect eleventh-century London from attack and, more important, to dominate the city both physically and visually. This point was made clear by historian William of Poitiers, who commented that King William temporarily departed London "while certain fortifications were completed in the city against the restlessness of the vast and fierce populace for he [William] realized that it was of the first importance to overawe the Londoners."[9]

In 1250, the White Tower was further fortified by a high stone wall called the Ballium Wall with thirteen towers and a double drawbridge entry. Thirty years later, a second outer wall was added with eight towers and a great moat twenty-five feet wide and eleven feet deep filled with water.

During the late thirteenth century, more functions were added to the

Beefeaters

The Beefeaters at the Tower of London were originally established in 1485 as King Henry VIII's bodyguards. They are perhaps best known for their elegant scarlet and gold uniforms that date to 1552. Worn on state occasions, the uniform consists of a knee-length scarlet tunic, scarlet knee breeches and stockings, and a round brimmed hat called a Tudor bonnet. Queen Elizabeth recently introduced the distinctive white neck ruff worn by them. When on duty, each guard is armed with an eight-foot-long pike known as a partisan. The chief warder carries a staff surmounted by a silver model of the White Tower and is paid 6d. a day; his second-in-command, the yeoman gaoler, possesses a ceremonial ax and is paid 4d. a day.

The Beefeaters are warders of the Tower of London and hold the keys to it.

Although the Beefeaters are officially called yeoman's warders, many different stories explain the more popular term *Beefeaters*. One story suggests that the name derives from the kings allowing yeoman's warders to eat the remains of their dinners. Another claims that they were allowed to eat as much beef as they could fit on the blade of a dagger. Yet a third story says that the term may originally have been derogatory, used by the lower classes in sneering at the "pampered guards" who regularly ate beef while they rarely had any.

Edward Wessex describes the ceremonial locking of the Tower in his book *Crown and Country: A Personal Guide to Royal London*. Every night at 9:53, the Beefeaters perform the "Ceremony of the Keys" to lock the Tower for the night. The chief warder marches outside and shouts, "An escort for the keys." Four armed guards join him and the main gates are locked. They then assemble and are confronted by a sentry, at which time the following exchange takes place:

"Halt, who goes there?"

The Chief Warder replies, "The Keys."

"Whose keys?"

"King James' keys."

"God preserve King James!"

The whole guard replies, "Amen!"

The Tower of London is the city's most imposing monument and its most captivating tourist attraction.

Tower. Because it was already well fortified and well guarded, it was the obvious candidate to become the royal mint, the royal storage house of records, and a prison. Shortly thereafter, the Tower also became the repository for the Crown Jewels, which were moved from Westminster Abbey.

Next on the itinerary is St. Paul's Cathedral, located in London's West End, within the city walls. It is a long walk from the Tower, but since the Tower is just three blocks from the river, proceed to the dock and catch a westward wherry to Anchor Wharf. Upon arrival, walk north four blocks to Ludgate Street and you will see the towering cathedral.

St. Paul's Cathedral

Religion has always played a major role in the lives of the English. The current St. Paul's Cathedral is the fourth building to occupy this plot of hallowed ground. The first cathedral to stand here was erected in A.D. 604 and dedicated to St. Paul, the patron saint of London. The wooden church, which was built by King Ethelbert of Kent, the first Christian king of England, was destroyed by fire in 675, but rebuilt between 675 and 685. Fire was not the only danger that this great cathedral faced in those dark centuries of Saxon England. The Vikings destroyed the second St. Paul's in 962 during one of their periodic invasions, but it was immediately rebuilt.

The size of St. Paul's Cathedral makes it a must-see for sightseers.

London Castles

Castles in London, such as the Tower, are built to serve many functions, not just for those living in them but for the surrounding population as well, who depend on castles as a place of safety in times of disturbance. For this reason, every castle has specific architectural features that protect it from invasions. The most important features are the keep, bailey, moat, and drawbridge.

The keep is a self-contained tall tower that functions as both a residence and a defense structure. The lord or king can live, eat meals, and sleep here. In times of peril, soldiers occupy the top turrets to drive off an invading enemy. The majority of keeps are two or three stories tall, made of thick stone walls to withstand battering rams and fires, and have only a few narrow windows to admit light yet prevent an enemy from squeezing through.

The bailey is a large area of several acres that is usually surrounded by a moat. In addition to many buildings, it includes a large grassy area for various events, such as festivals, sporting events, gatherings of the castle guards, and executions.

The moat that surrounds the bailey is usually a great mound of earth with a deep ditch in front of it that prevents invaders from entering the bailey. If a castle is located near a plentiful source of water, the ditch is flooded to provide a more effective barrier than a dry moat.

The drawbridge is usually the only way one can cross over the moat and enter the bailey. Drawbridges are hinged on the bottom of the inner side and by chains attached to the outer side. By using pulleys, the drawbridge can be raised to a vertical position, preventing anyone from crossing the moat, or lowered to allow people to enter.

The castle of the Tower of London is both a royal residence and a structure for defense.

In 1087, following one of London's many fires that destroyed the third St. Paul's, construction began again, but this time the cathedral was constructed of stone blocks transported across the English Channel from Normandy, France, the home of William the Conqueror. After a little more than 150 years, the final touches were applied to the 596-foot-long structure in 1240, completing the largest cathedral in Europe. It also boasted the tallest spire at 489 feet. Today, 364 years later, St. Paul's is the third largest cathedral in Europe.

St. Paul's is shaped like a cross: Its 596-foot-long floor is intersected in the middle by a transept. The entry to St. Paul's is in the center of the long floor. Once inside, the great hall to the left, the *Navis Ecclesia,* is cavernous, the ceiling being supported by twenty-four stone piers. To the right of the entry is the *Chorus Ecclesia,* where wanderers will find several small altars and private places of worship. Although the walls have many small windows, the interior is quite dark, which is why during Sunday services visitors will see several hundred lit candles.

Visitors may notice damage to the open-air pulpit along St. Paul's south wall. The damage is the result of lingering religious friction between members of the Church of England and the Catholic Church. Sermons inciting Londoners to riot did just that. They rampaged the interior, destroying the high altar and several old tombs, and burned tapestries hanging on the walls. Regardless of the recent misfortune, St.

Westminster Hall (right) is one of the most magnificent structures along the Thames River.

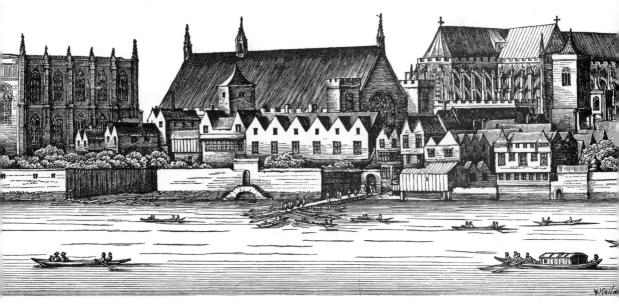

port Parliament Stairs. From there, the palace is straight ahead on the bank of the river.

Westminster Palace

Westminster Palace can be easily found on the Thames in the district of Westminster where the river makes its sweeping right angle to the south. Westminster Palace was the second great structure built by William the Conqueror after the Tower. Its original use was as the official residence for the king and his family, and it functioned as such until 1512. The first king to live here on a full-time basis was William's son, King William II. William II built the adjoining Westminster Hall, which is located at the northern end of the palace. Westminster Palace is large and intricate. Its buildings contain nearly twelve hundred rooms, one hundred staircases, and well over two miles of passages.

Most impressive of all the halls and rooms at the palace is Westminster Hall, more commonly called the Great Hall because of its dimensions. It is 290 feet long and 68 feet wide, with ceiling structures rising 92 feet above the floor. When it was built, the Great Hall was the largest in Europe. Originally designed as a place for feasting and entertaining, the hall's size later made it an ideal meeting place for Parliament as well.

The wood-beam ceiling of Westminster Hall reminds many visitors of the interior of a wooden ship.

Paul's is the largest and oldest place of worship in London and remains a favorite landmark for sightseers.

The third stop on the tour of historical monuments is Westminster Palace, best known as the palace where Parliament meets. From St. Paul's, wander back to the Thames and catch another wherry westward to the water

Until the late thirteenth century, Westminster Palace functioned exclusively as the royal palace. But in 1295, King Edward I convened the first official meeting of Parliament. Parliament, from the French word *parler*, meaning "to speak," is the advisory council made up of nobility, including bishops of the church, knights, and barons. Parliament only convenes when the sovereign calls the members, and it ends when they are dismissed. Queen Elizabeth, for example, convened Parliament only thirteen times during her forty-five-year reign.

The magnificent hammer-beam roof of the Great Hall, originally supported by two interior rows of pillars, was designed during the reign of Richard II. This elegant wood-beam ceiling is often compared to the wood ribs found in the structural interior of a wooden

A view of the Northern Transept of Westminster Abbey. No visitor to London should miss this beautiful historic landmark.

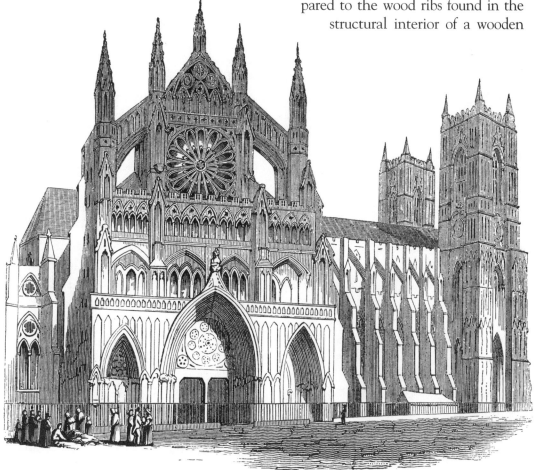

ship. In fact, it may be that carpenters schooled in shipbuilding were involved in the construction.

To the east and south of the hall are the apartments of the palace used by the royal family and the royal chapel of St. Stephen. Kings worship in the upper chapel, while their courtiers worship in the lower level or "crypt" chapel below.

Upon exiting the palace, a short walk across the street away from the river will deliver tourists to the front steps of Westminster Abbey, the most visited monument in London.

Westminster Abbey

An architectural masterpiece built between the thirteenth and sixteenth centuries, Westminster Abbey is a favorite for Londoners as well as tourists. Westminster Abbey has long been associated with royalty as the place of their coronations and their tombs. If vacationers have only one or two days in the city, this is one of the most impressive historic landmarks worthy of a visit.

As visitors enter the abbey through the central door, they will see the massive main piers of the church that are made of marble, as are the floors. Structurally, the church remains as Henry III planned it, although the outside has been resurfaced. There are carvings and statuary throughout the building. On the left side of the entry rests a memorial built for Henry III. Made in Italy, it is richly adorned with a mosaic that is surmounted with a golden receptacle. According to legend, this receptacle holds the head of St. Benedict, a tooth of St. Anthanasius, some clothes of St. Peter, and a piece of cloth belonging to the Virgin Mary.

The history of the abbey began in 1050 when Edward the Confessor, a rather remote English king, sought to enlarge a Benedictine monastery close to his palace in Westminster and dedicate it to St. Peter. Tragically, when the church was dedicated in 1065, Edward was ill and could not attend the ceremony. Within a few days, he was dead. His body is entombed behind the high altar bearing this inscription:

> Edward the Confessor built the great Abbey church at this site. His body still rests here in this shrine which Henry III caused to be erected in 1268. And here, as FOUNDER OF WESTMINSTER ABBEY, his memory has ever been held in honour and grateful remembrance.[10]

While at the high altar, wander just west of Edward's tomb. Here, you will find eight kings and queens who are buried in the abbey, including Queen Elizabeth.

CHAPTER FIVE

Casual Sightseeing

I f visiting London's major architectural monuments has exhausted you, this might be a good time to relax for a day of casual sightseeing. London has many tranquil places of beauty that are enjoyable, educational, and fun. Recommended for a full day of touring are Eton College, London Bridge, the Globe Theatre, and the district of Greenwich. If they are visited in this order, the day's outing will begin west of London and finish a few miles east of the city.

Eton College

For vacationers interested in the academic achievement of the very rich, a twenty-mile westward boat ride will deliver academicians to the doorstep of London's most beautiful and prestigious campus, Eton College. Founded in 1440 by Henry VI as the King's College of Our Lady of Eton, the school is a picturesque place to visit. King Henry lavished on Eton not only a substantial amount of money but also a huge collection of holy relics.

Visitors to the college can vicariously experience the educational lives of England's most elite young gentlemen. Three hundred aristocratic boys from all over England attend Eton at no cost to their families. All the boys, who are between the ages of thirteen and seventeen, study here before moving on to one of England's foremost universities in Oxford, Cambridge, or London. Teaching them are a faculty of forty instructors called fellows specializing in the Greek and Latin languages, law, theology, business, medicine, and philosophy.

Although the young men come from wealthy families, their life at Eton is austere. They sleep two or three to a bed in Long Chamber, rise at 5:00 A.M., chant prayers while they dress, and are at class by 6:00. They are then marched in double file to College Hall for the first of the two meals of the day, except on Friday, a day of fasting when no meals are served. All instruction is in Latin, and classes finish at 8:00 in the evening, at which time the boys go to bed, again saying their prayers. The only break from studies occurs at noon when the students play soccer for one hour. The boys enjoy only two holidays each year: three weeks at Christmas, during which they must remain at Eton, and three weeks in the summer, when they may travel home.

Sightseers will find the campus to be a beautiful place to visit. The new church is quite impressive, as is the classroom along the north side of the schoolyard that was completed in 1443. Because all the students live on campus, visitors can see their dormitories, located on the north side of the schoolyard, and the accommodations for the fellows, who also live on campus at Cloister Court.

A view of Eton College from across the Thames. Apart from being one of the finest centers of learning in Europe, Eton is a charming place to visit.

London Bridge welcomes visitors with an unbroken row of shops along its span.

London Bridge

Smack in the center of London is one of the most fascinating structures to add to any sightseer's list, London Bridge. The only bridge crossing the Thames, London Bridge was begun around the year 1176 and completed in 1209. Building in the middle of the swift-moving Thames River was dangerous work; 150 workmen died by being crushed under falling blocks of stone or drowned.

Before beginning a walk across the bridge, take a few moments on the wharf to study its ornaments. The most dominant feature is the colorful three- and four-story wooden shops that occupy the entire length of the bridge. There are forty buildings altogether, set into four groups of about ten shops each. The gaps between each cluster enable larger

The Great Stone Gates

While crossing the London Bridge, be sure to notice its most ominous feature, the stone gate at each end. Built and positioned for the defense of the city, each has a massive oak door and a portcullis, a heavy iron gate that can be dropped down through slots to the walkway below, preventing enemies from crossing the bridge. The great stone gates tell a history of London that cannot be found anywhere else. These gates, which function primarily to protect London, acquired a second, far more infamous reputation as the place where the heads of traitors are impaled on pikes. Sometimes as many as thirty heads at a time can be seen acting as deterrents to others who may think about betraying the city.

The custom of impaling heads began during the fourteenth century when groups of criminals and political enemies of the king tried to sneak across the bridge to invade London. When they were caught, they were beheaded. Their severed heads were impaled on twenty-foot pikes and placed above the towers for all entering or exiting the city to see. Over time, the heads shriveled and fell into the Thames.

The most unusual story about a head placed here involves Sir Thomas More, whose refusal to support King Henry VIII resulted in his execution in 1535. His head was said to have stayed on the bridge for months in a pristine state, without a trace of decomposition, before it was eventually reclaimed by his family.

At times the gateway to the Bloody Tower on London Bridge is used to display the heads of traitors on pikes.

vehicles to pass each other on the bridge. The buildings' lively colors attract shoppers and sightseers from miles around. Many vividly colored pennants also float above the shops, lending a festive air to the bridge. In 1572, German travelers Georg Braun and Franz Hogenberg noted both the bridge and the shops: "A stone bridge leads over to the other side of the river, a long and amazing work constructed on a series of arches, with houses on both sides of it arranged so that it does not look like a bridge but a continuous street."[11]

The many fires that have ravaged London over the years prompted merchants to build their shops on the bridge because it was in the middle of the Thames and was made of stone. Merchants saw the bridge as a place safe from fire. Although the bridge is twenty feet wide and was able to accommodate carts passing in each direction when it was new, now there is scarcely room for one cart at a time to travel down the center.

The shops on the bridge are made of timber frames with plaster walls. They are stabilized on the bridge by support beams bolted to the stone piers supporting the walkway. The shops on either side are linked by third-story walkways. Even though the stone bridge is safe from fire, the shops are not. Fires have broken out on several occasions, requiring the rebuilding of all wooden structures.

The bridge is built on nineteen stone piers in the river, none of which is the same distance apart. Each pier was formed by driving a ring of elm pilings into the riverbed, filling the area inside with rubble, and then laying a floor of oak beams over the arches between the piers. Over the years, the width of the piers has been extended. As a result, the flow of the river is very restricted under the bridge, causing the current to be very fast. Many people have lost their lives trying to navigate small boats between the pilings.

As travelers wander across the bridge, they will find a few structures other than the shops. On the ninth pier out from the city is a chapel dedicated to the memory of St. Thomas à Becket, the archbishop of Canterbury, who was murdered in Canterbury Cathedral by assassins sent by King Henry II. This cathedral was built sometime during the twelfth century and was renovated two hundred years later.

Boat traffic up and down the Thames required the construction of a drawbridge. The drawbridge section, which still stands in the center of the bridge, once allowed tall masted ships to pass through the bridge. In 1550, however, the mechanically operated winches used to open the bridge failed and were never repaired. Consequently, tall ships arriving from Europe today cannot proceed past the bridge.

To provide security for the city, a great stone gate was built at each end of the bridge. Each contains a wooden door and an iron gate that can be shut at a moment's notice in case of a civil disturbance. These gates are also closed each night when the curfew bell sounds.

After studying the mechanics of the south gate of the bridge, continue south into the district of Southwark and find your way four blocks down Great Surrey Street. Then go two blocks to the right on Stamford to the Globe Theatre.

The Globe Theatre

A visit to the Globe Theatre, London's largest, is a ritual for all theatergoers and for visitors interested in architecture and literature. Completed just five years ago in 1599 by brothers Richard and Cuthbert Burbage, this circular theater accommodates three thousand spectators.

Visitors approaching the theater will immediately recognize it because of its cylindrical shape and thatched gallery roof made of straw.

On days when plays are produced, the Globe flies a large colorful banner from the roof to attract customers. During an off day, anyone can enter the theater to have a look around at no cost. Upon entry, proceed directly to the open courtyard where the stage stands. From here, the theater will seem small,

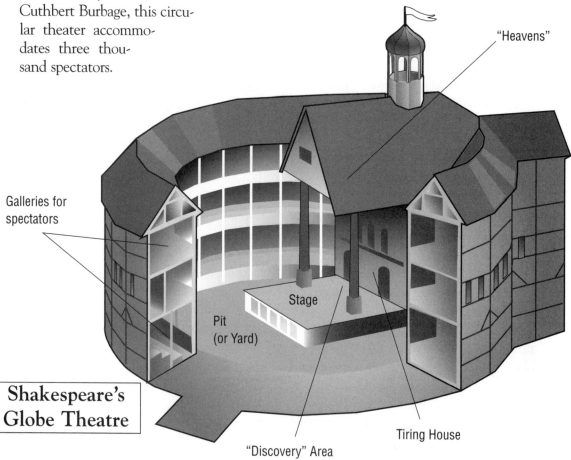

"Heavens"

Galleries for spectators

Stage

Pit (or Yard)

Tiring House

Shakespeare's Globe Theatre

"Discovery" Area

The *Golden Hind*

The beautiful flagship of Sir Francis Drake, the *Golden Hind*, is currently tied up at the wharf in Greenwich. This presents foreign visitors with a rare opportunity to experience one of England's most famous galleons. This three-masted ship—two main masts and one secondary—is eighty-eight feet long, twenty feet wide, and seventy feet to the top of the main masts. It is a square-rigger sailing ship, meaning that its four main sails are square.

The *Golden Hind* functions as both a warship and a transport ship, and its construction meets both needs. Its sides are made of four-foot-thick hard oak planking capable of absorbing two-hundred-pound cannon balls fired at point-blank range. As for its own defense, the *Golden Hind* is outfitted with twenty cannons, all of which can be seen protruding along each side on the second of the ship's five decks. The heavy oak planking along with the cannons, artifacts, masts, and riggings and fittings weigh 120 tons. But despite its heavy weight for fighting sea battles, it is remarkably fast, capable of managing five to six knots in fair winds and even faster in strong ones. However, these galleons are top-heavy, and in high seas running at high speeds, they can easily capsize.

Francis Drake's ship the Golden Hind *can be seen docked at Portsmouth Wharf.*

The poop deck at the stern of the ship has recently been repainted, and the bright colors are added for this exhibition only. The name of the ship is proudly painted above the rudder, part of which protrudes from the water because the ship is lighter than when it sails. The original name of Drake's ship was the *Pelican*, but he changed it to the *Golden Hind* in 1577 in honor of the figure of a golden deer that appears on the coat-of-arms of Lord C.C. Hatton, who financed the ship's circumnavigation of the globe.

just one hundred feet in diameter and thirty-six feet from the floor to the open-air roof. Although most Londoners describe the interior as a circle, it is actually a twenty-four-sided building. Gazing around the all-wood interior, the three-tiered galleries along the edge of the walls that surround the stage accommodate the wealthier patrons who can afford seats. These three galleries are stacked straight up from the floor, one on top of the other, and are supported by heavy beams that some theatergoers complain about because they obstruct their views of the stage.

Those who are unable to afford the price of a seat are charged one penny to watch from the standing room on the ground floor of the gallery, often called the pit, immediately in front of the stage. The standing room area is fifteen feet deep from the edge of the stage. The five-foot-tall stage is made of wood and is fifty feet from side to side. The spaces under and behind the stage are used for special effects, storage, and costume changes.

Greenwich

Greenwich is a lovely area enjoyed by many Londoners, located about three miles east of the Globe. It is said to have been called *Grenovicum* by the Romans; later, the Saxon term was *Grenewic*, meaning the "green village." Today, Greenwich is the site of beautiful royal castles, green parks, walkways along the Thames, and England's most famous ship, the *Golden Hind*, which is on public display.

One of London's most beautiful royal palaces, Greenwich Palace, the birthplace of King Henry VIII and Queen Elizabeth, is located here. For many years, this was the place where ceremonies and balls entertaining many of Europe's royalty were held. During King Henry VIII's reign, it was also a popular spot for jousting tournaments and royal boat regattas on the Thames.

A walk around this beautiful estate is a favorite outing for Londoners, who enjoy the palace, the verdant grounds surrounding it, and the carefully maintained walks around the exterior. Although commoners cannot enter the palace, on a sunny day this is a perfect location for a picnic lunch, providing a spectacular view of the Thames.

Following a walk around the grounds, a short walk to the boat docks will allow visitors to view and board England's most famous ship. When Sir Francis Drake returned here after his thirty-six thousand mile trip, Queen Elizabeth knighted him on the decks of the ship and then provided a gala dinner ceremony. To celebrate the occasion, Drake decorated the ship in brightly colored banners that still fly from its masts.

Eton, London Bridge, the Globe, and Greenwich are a few of the attractions for which London is famous. However, they are by no means the only ones. For tourists, shopping is as much an attraction as sightseeing. London has a variety of unique items available, and shopping here is made simpler by clever city planning.

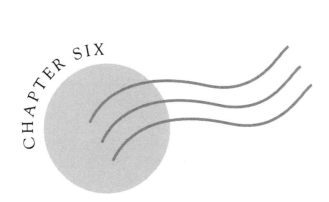

CHAPTER SIX

Shopping

London is a shopper's paradise. Not only does the city provide as exceptional an assortment of rare and beautiful goods as any major city in Europe, but its carefully planned and organized shopping districts help shoppers locate them. One of the city's leading importers commented on London and the goods its shops have to offer: It is "the chiefest emporium, or town of trade in the world; the largest and most populous, the fairest and most opulent city at this day in all Europe, perhaps the whole world."[12]

For visitors, street names are the first indication of where they can find whatever they are looking for. The main street for purchasing inexpensive groceries and other merchandise is Cheapside Street, the widest and most important street for shopping in London. Locals refer to it as simply "the street." In the immediate vicinity of Cheapside are Poultry Street, Milk Street, Bread Street,

and Old Fish Street. Other street names describing the wares they sell include Grocers' Court, Candlestick Lane, Apple Yard, Shoe Lane, Frying Pan Alley, and Bank Side.

Another convenience provided to visitors is the city's several locations of clusters of shops. The two most interesting and most highly recommended are Cheapside Street and the Royal Exchange.

Cheapside Street

Cheapside Street is the city's largest commercial street, running the length of the city from the west-side city wall at Newgate to the east-side wall at Aldgate. Cheapside is more accurately described as a marketplace than a street carrying traffic. This commercial street is different from others because all the shops are temporary stalls that are set up in the morning and disassembled at night. The stalls consist of wood corner-posts covered by colorful canopies. This allows the shops to be removed at a moment's notice if the lord mayor of London suddenly wishes to use the street as a place for a jousting tournament or a public execution, which he occasionally does.

Cheapside is a lively mix of foreign and local shoppers jostling one another amid the shouts of shop owners vying for their attention. Ned Ward, who visited Cheapside, commented on the overly aggressive nature of some owners:

I was suddenly accosted by a parcel of nimble-tongued sinners who leaped out of their shops, and swarmed around me like so many bees about a honeysuckle. Some got me by the hands, some by the elbows, others by the shoulders, and made such a din in my ears, that I thought I had committed some egregious trespass unawares, and they had seized me as a prisoner. They hustled me backwards and forwards like a pickpocket in a crowd, till at last I made loose and scampered like a restless prisoner from a gang of bailiffs.[13]

The din and general commotion found at Cheapside make for a colorful day unlike

The market at Cheapside provides an enticing way to spend an afternoon. Rows of wooden stalls have for sale virtually every type of commodity imaginable.

The Royal Exchange offers discriminating shoppers an unparalleled experience. The building includes more than one hundred shops, filled with fine goods from around the globe.

that experienced at any of London's other shopping areas. Here, tourists can wander through a mile of stalls selling everything imaginable. Foods from England and Europe include such things as fresh fruit and vegetables, chunks of beef, cheeses and wines from France, freshly cut flowers, and squirming fish destined for taverns and the homes of the wealthy. Fresh fish is so important that when a fish is sold, the fish-mongers slit open its belly, placing the guts into the hands of the pur-chaser to show whether the pike was sufficiently fat and fresh, and then the belly [is] sewed up again: if the pike prove[s] good enough, then the purchaser [takes] it, but if the guts look thin and poor the fishmonger [keeps] it, throwing it back in the basin to be eaten by the other fish.[14]

Even the bizarre is for sale. Buttons made of human teeth and boots removed from the feet of executed criminals have both been found here.

The Royal Exchange

For avid shoppers with a crown or two in their purses looking for a shopping experience more sophisticated than that on Cheapside Street, there is nothing like the Royal Exchange anywhere in the world, not even in Paris. Located on Threadneedle Street, this unusual group of shops contained within one building was conceived and built in 1566 by Sir Thomas Gresham, and so impressed Queen Elizabeth that she officially named it the Royal Exchange. First-time visitors will immediately recognize the four-story brick building by the green grasshopper, the Gresham family crest, which sits on top of the building's bell tower.

Shoppers looking for fine knife blades should visit one of London's many blade smiths in London's ironworkers' district, just north of Cheapside.

Dueling

For foreign visitors to London who wish to carry a sword, a word of caution is in order. Dueling is illegal. Drawing a sword is also illegal unless a crime is in progress and there is a legitimate need for protection. Anyone wishing to settle a personal grudge is advised to do so in France or in some other city. The issue of reckless sword use, commonly called swordplay, is often the result of too much ale and too little restraint. Calling someone a liar, or otherwise impugning his honor, his courage, or his name is a challenge in itself. Nowhere is the foolishness of swordplay better described than by Lawrence Stone in his book *Crisis of the Aristocracy:* "Tempers were short and weapons easy to hand. The basic characteristics of the nobility, like those of the poor, were ferocity, childishness, and lack of self control."

In the event that an insult is spoken and a duel appears inevitable, the recommended response is to try to avoid the fight if possible with apologies from both sides. If, however, someone new to London finds a duel unavoidable, knowing the rules of swordplay as they are practiced here will come in handy. Unlike in France, for example, where group duels often occur, in London a duel involves only two adversaries.

Since fights to the death are common, never allow an adversary who falls down to regain his footing or allow a person who drops his sword to pick it up. If either of these circumstances occurs, the fallen or disarmed man must be given an opportunity to apologize and to ask for mercy. If he does, the victor must allow him to leave dishonored but without his sword. If no apology is given, the man with the advantage is expected to continue the fight to the death. Although some believe it to be gentlemanly to allow a fallen adversary to regain his footing or a dropped sword to be picked up, it is in fact a mistake.

If a deep wound is inflicted and much blood appears, the stricken man must be given an opportunity to apologize and to beg for mercy. In such a case, the adversary must accept the apology and allow the dishonored man to depart. If a light wound is inflicted, however, and the stricken man begs for mercy, the request must be denied and the duel continued.

The revolutionary feature of this unique store is that shoppers are able to visit one hundred different shops without leaving the building. This means no getting wet walking up and down streets, no need to worry about being trampled by reckless horse and carriage drivers, and no irritation of noisy and smelly streets. The Royal Exchange is pure shopping pleasure for the fashion-conscious capable of affording the very best. Bernard de Mandeville, a French visitor, summed up the importance of dressing well by observing,

Handsome apparel is the main point, fine feathers make fine birds and people, where they are not known, are generally honour'd according to their clothes and other accoutrements they have on them; from the richness of them we judge their wealth. It is this which encourages everybody, who is conscious of his merit, if he is any ways able, to wear clothes above his rank.[15]

Once inside, well-heeled shoppers will find goldsmiths, booksellers, seamstresses, armorers, apothecaries, glassblow-ers, dress shops, spice shops, candle shops, porcelain makers, silk fabrics, and dozens of other curiosities. The Royal Exchange's daily hours are from 7:00 A.M. to 7:00 P.M.

Swords of every type are readily available in London. But be forewarned; although gentlemen resort to swords to settle questions of honor, reckless swordplay such as that depicted here is highly illegal.

Swords

Swords are worn on the streets of London by gentlemen as a sign of status and as a statement of personal protection. Since London does not have a police force like the one in Paris, gentlemen from time to time draw their swords to chase off thieves or to settle arguments. Because of their wide use, London is an ideal location to purchase swords. Just north of Cheapside Street on Lothbury, shoppers will hear the deafening racket of hammers striking anvils and smell the hot metal in white-hot forges. This is the ironworkers' district and it is a dirty, noisy, and smelly place that announces itself for several blocks in all directions.

Sword makers specialize in custom-making the most popular types of weapons found in London today: the English long sword, the rapier, the broadsword, and the dagger. Once a style is chosen, the buyer will then specify the precise weight, length, hilt (handle) design, quillon (protective cross-guard above the hilt), scabbard (sheath), and engraving, if desired.

The English long sword is a two-handed weapon made popular by Henry VIII that is still seen from time to time on London streets. It is a double-edged sword used in sweeping, powerful hacking motions meant to slash an opponent's left side, the *mandritta*, or his right side, the *riversi*. Its considerable length, five to six feet, and weight, however, make it cumbersome for everyday use. The size necessitates carrying it pointing straight

A wide variety of fashions are available in London. However, shoppers should take note of English sumptuary laws, restricting particular fabrics to particular social classes.

tlemen carry two rapiers, one for each hand, both of which are carried in a single scabbard.

The broadsword is a hybrid of the English long sword and the rapier. It is a double-edged sword, typically forty to forty-eight inches long, but light enough to be used in one hand. It does not possess a sharp point, limiting its use to quick slashing at the sides of an enemy's body or neck.

The dagger is the most dangerous of the swords because it is small, twelve to eighteen inches, and is wielded very quickly. Dagger users typically hold the weapon in the right hand and some object in the left hand to distract the enemy, such as a small shield or a cloak—hence the popular term *cloak and dagger*.

Cost will be a function of sword type, quality, and detail. Buyers should expect to pay between an angel and a sovereign. Because of the time involved in custom-forging a sword, the buyer will need to return several days after ordering it.

High Fashion

London enjoys an international reputation among stylish women for *haute couture*, a commonly used French term mean-

up in the left hand against the shoulder to keep the right hand rested and ready to join the left in case of a fight.

If the buyer prefers a lighter, quicker sword, the rapier is an excellent and very popular choice. Forty-two to forty-eight inches long, the rapier is a double-edged sword that also has a sharp tip for inflicting deep puncture wounds. Some London gening "high fashion." Many of London's most expensive shops cater to women interested in the latest and finest quality dresses, shoes, hats, and accessories. The best shops can be found on Lombard Street, at the Royal Exchange, and at shops on the London Bridge.

For shoppers new to London, it is important to be aware of the sumptuary laws passed by King Henry VIII regulating the extravagance, luxury, and costs of clothing. The king was not attempting to outlaw such clothing, but wanted to limit particular

Coats of arms like this one, are symbolic representations of animals and figures particular to a family. A coat of arms remains one of the most popular tourist purchases in London.

types of clothing to particular social classes. He wanted to be able to determine a person's social class by simply glancing at his or her clothes. A few examples of the restrictions are the following:

> None shall wear cloth of gold or silver, or silk of purple color except Countesses and all above that rank. None shall wear silk or cloth mixed with or embroidered with silk, pearls, gold or silver except Baronesses and all above that rank. None shall wear cloth of silver in belts except wives of Knights and all above that rank.[16]

The latest fashions feature tight-waisted dresses with corsets and full skirts made out of silk and trimmed with lace. Sleeves reach the wrist even in summer and are lined with fur and folded back past the elbow to reveal the expensive lining. Dresses and skirts are also long, usually reaching the floor. To shape skirts and give them the desired fit, women wear a farthingale underneath made of wire loops. Many women are also wearing a constricting corset of leather or thin wood to flatten their breasts. The corset allows evening gowns to have square necklines that are low cut yet not too revealing.

Besides elaborate dresses and skirts, accessories are popular items. Every woman wears something on her head, usually a hood or decorated hat. Neck ruffs, three-inch-thick lace-trimmed circular collars, are a necessity for every fashionable woman. The "bumroll," a crescent-shaped pad that ties around the waist with the thickest part resting on the backside, has also become very popular. The bumroll makes the waist more appealing by increasing the bulk toward the back and then tapering toward the front.

Coats of Arms

Coats of arms are a popular purchase for English visitors to London, as well as for many from France, Germany, and Italy. The origin of coats of arms is vague, but some authorities believe that they began many centuries ago as symbols painted on shields and articles of clothing to identify members of feudal armies during battle. Other authorities think that they grew out of the use of signet rings; gentlemen of the time would use a personal seal stamped in wax alongside their name as positive identification.

Whatever the origin might be, the use of coats of arms continues today in warfare and as a form of decoration for display in homes, shops, on saddles and stationery, and embroidered on clothing and scarves. Several well-qualified painters in London will reproduce a family's coat of arms in true detail and color on a canvas banner or wooden sign of any size. Be aware, however, that some of these painters will require proof of legitimate use before beginning a reproduction; a coat of arms can only be awarded by the king. To provide proof, the coat of arms must be officially registered in the College of Arms, sometimes called the Herald's College, which was established in 1483 by King Richard III because of the need to limit their use and ensure that each coat of arms is unique.

Although a coat of arms itself cannot be purchased, those who have been granted the right to display one can have it designed here or, if it already exists, reproduced. Generally, the designer of the coat of arms selects the colors; a main symbol such as an animal or other object; various vertical, horizontal, or diagonal stripes; and possibly a motto emblazoned on the bottom.

Designers of coats of arms claim that symbols and colors have meaning. For example, the lion denotes great courage; the horse, readiness to serve king and country; and the trumpet, readiness for a fight. As for colors, yellow denotes generosity; silver, sincerity; black, consistency; blue, truth; and red, strength in battle.

Once completed, the reproduction may be used by all immediate family members, but only sons inherit the right to display it when they leave the family. When a woman marries, she assumes the coat of arms of her husband's family.

After a long day of shopping, many vacationers may long to see some type of entertainment. London provides many entertaining activities—from dramatic plays at one of its many theaters to festivals and bear baiting.

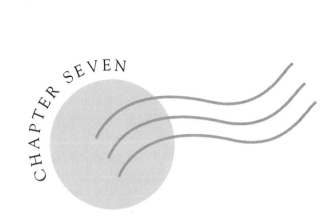

CHAPTER SEVEN

Entertainment

As any veteran traveler knows, shopping, sightseeing, and navigating in an unfamiliar large city can be exhausting. Fortunately for vacationers, London provides a wide assortment of entertaining activities that do not require much energy. After a few days of intense tourist activities, consider a day of rest at one of the many sites providing entertainment. For those who enjoy the theater, a finer city cannot be found.

Theater

No city in Europe can surpass the quality and quantity of dramatic theaters found in London. Londoners are proud of their many theaters and large pool of talented poets and playwrights. London has theaters that are indoors in small, intimate settings as well as larger, open-air theaters. No matter what time of year you visit, the city's theatrical groups are ready to cater to all dramatic preferences.

The Elizabethan era was an exciting time for London's theaters, and that excitement continues. Before Queen Elizabeth, London did not have buildings dedicated exclusively to theater. Troupes of actors performed in halls, courts, taverns, courtyards, and any other available open spaces. In 1574, however, the queen passed a law requiring theaters in London to be licensed, and in 1576 James Burbage built the first permanent theater called the Theatre, just outside the city walls.

Today, London has more than a dozen first-rate theaters throughout the city that print and post playbills announcing the plays, actors, and schedules. Since most of the major theaters such as the Rose, the Hope, the Theatre, the Globe, and the Swan are located across the river in Southwark close to the London Bridge, that is the recommended place to find a great play.

In 1596, three years before the construction of the Globe Theatre, the visiting architect Arend van Buchell commented, "There are four amphitheatres in London of notable beauty, which from their diverse signs bear diverse names [the Theatre, Curtain, Rose, and Swan]. In each of them a different play is daily exhibited to the populace."[17]

The largest theaters offer performances during the day to take advantage of the natural light that floods through their open-roofed ceilings. The price of a ticket depends whether the ticket buyer wishes to sit or stand. The best seats, located high around the gallery, will cost 6 to 8d. For that amount, spectators will be able to see the stage, hear the actors, and sit in relative safety. For one penny, a theatergoer can stand in the pit just in front of the stage. Although they are packed in, many mill about during the performances, get drunk on ale, eat chicken dinners, throw the bones, sometimes heckle the actors onstage, and occasionally start fights.

A great number of plays by popular playwrights are performed. Among the favorites are those by Thomas Sackville, Thomas Norton, Christopher Marlowe, Thomas Kyd, Ben Jonson, and, of course, William Shakespeare. When Thomas Platter visited London in 1599, he attended a Shakespearean play in the Globe Theatre and commented,

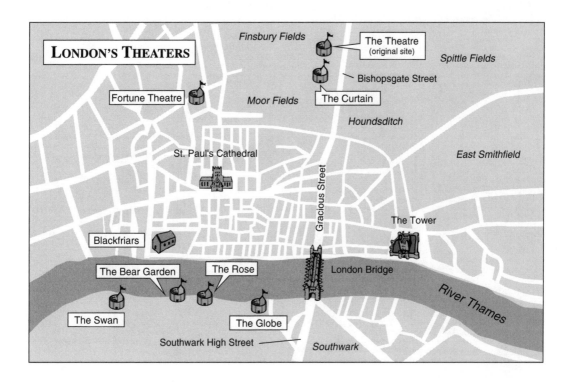

London's Theaters

Finsbury Fields
The Theatre (original site)
Spittle Fields
Bishopsgate Street
Fortune Theatre
Moor Fields
The Curtain
Houndsditch
St. Paul's Cathedral
East Smithfield
Gracious Street
The Tower
Blackfriars
The Bear Garden
The Rose
London Bridge
The Swan
The Globe
Southwark High Street
Southwark
River Thames

I and my party crossed the water [the Thames], and there in the house with the thatched roof [the Globe] witnessed an excellent performance of the Shakespearean tragedy of the first Emperor Julius Caesar with a cast of some fifteen people; when the play was over, they danced very marvelously and gracefully together as is their wont, two dressed as men and two [male actors] as women.[18]

The Lord Mayor's Festivals

Festivals in London occur throughout the year. Innkeepers are a good source of information for when and where festivals take place.

A view of the interior of an open-air theater. Depending on your budget, you may stand with the groundlings in the pit or sit in style with the nobility in the gallery.

William Shakespeare

Many visitors come to London to view the latest plays by one of the city's favorite playwrights, William Shakespeare. Born in 1564 in Stratford-upon-Avon, seventy-five miles northwest of London, where he attended the local school, Shakespeare enjoyed reading and attending the local theater when traveling theatrical troops came through.

By 1588, Shakespeare had arrived in London to improve his craft and six years later established a good reputation as a playwright and actor. With two patrons providing him with financial assistance, Shakespeare rose quickly in the theater, as is evidenced by the elegant home he purchased a few years ago in Stratford.

Today, Shakespeare is widely regarded as one of London's best young playwrights, and some even think the best ever. He has written numerous plays, some of which are very comical, some tragic, and some of historical interest. Besides his plays, he has also published many of the most beautiful sonnets in the English language. Much of his success has been his ability to create characters that convey a thorough understanding of human behavior and everyday interactions of the lowborn as well as the highborn.

Shakespeare was a favorite of Queen Elizabeth and most likely will be for King James as well. Shakespeare's most recent popular plays that are currently produced at the Globe Theatre and elsewhere are the histories *Henry VI, Parts I, II,* and *III, Henry IV, Parts I* and *II,* and *Richard III;* the comedies *A Midsummer Night's Dream, Much Ado About Nothing, As You Like It,* and *Twelfth Night;* and the tragedies *Romeo and Juliet, Julius Caesar, King Lear,* and *Hamlet.*

William Shakespeare has become one of London's leading playwrights since coming to London in 1588.

Travelers fortunate to be in the city on the first day of March may attend the annual procession that officially marks the beginning of the term of office for the lord mayor of London. This colorful extravaganza begins at St. Paul's Cathedral and proceeds to Westminster Palace and back. The event is a fun-filled day honoring the newly chosen lord mayor and the twenty-six aldermen of London. The first leg of the procession parades from St. Paul's down to the docks, where it boards barges for the trip to Westminster Palace. The barges are colorfully decorated, bearing flags and banners. Accompanying barges carry musicians who entertain the officials as well as the hundreds of private boats and wherries hired by citizens enjoying the flotilla on the river.

When the entourage of boats reaches Westminster Palace, the participants disembark and proceed to the palace, where the lord mayor takes his oath of office. Following the ceremony, the people return to their boats and to the wharf for the main parade. The officials parade up Bridge Street to Ludgate Street and on to St. Paul's. One of the most enjoyable aspects of the parade is the array of floats. Each float has a theme, such as celebrations of London, commerce, honor, obeying laws, and loyalty to the Crown.

When the parade is over, the officials and participants convene at the Guidhall in the City of London, where they enjoy a feast paid for by the lord mayor.

Frost Fair

Visitors in London during the winter months may find the Thames frozen for short periods. Although the ice makes boat transportation impossible, there is one benefit: the Frost Fair that is held a quarter-mile east of the London Bridge directly on the frozen river. This fair is organized by the watermen to raise money as compensation for their lost wages while the river remains frozen.

The watermen erect stalls that stretch from side to side, flying colorful pennants to attract shoppers. This is an ideal place to purchase small, inexpensive handicrafts, pastries, flowers, and jewelry. Hot food, such as roasted ox, is sold each day. In addition, musicians, jugglers, and other street entertainers are on hand. Sports on the ice, including archery contests, ball games, and ice bowling matches, are also a major attraction.

Greyhound Racing

A popular sporting activity in London is greyhound racing. The popularity of greyhound racing prompted the queen to appoint the duke of Norfolk to draw up formal rules for this new competitive sport.

Greyhound racing does not take place in a stadium but in the fields outside of the city wall, where dog owners, bettors, and race officials meet. The rules specify that there be three officials: the hare-finder, respon-

A view of the Frost Fair on the frozen Thames. With its numerous attractions, the fair draws many visitors to London in the winter.

sible for finding and flushing the hare from the bushes; the fewterer, the dog handler who undoes the leashes, allowing the dogs to chase the hare; and the formal judge, responsible for determining the winner.

A race begins with all parties mounting their horses and following the hare-finder and fewterer holding the leashes of the two chosen dogs. As the entourage moves through the fields and the hare-finder flushes a hare, he yells out three times "So How" to alert the fewterer. When the fewterer locates the hare and sees that it has a head start of eighty yards, he slips the leashes off the dogs and the race is on. As the dogs pursue the hare at a top speed of thirty miles an hour, the spectators on horses thunder after

them across streams and sometimes through the crops of local farmers, destroying them as they run. Riders are compelled by the rules to remain at least forty yards behind the dogs. If a rider accidentally tramples a dog, he must pay the owner for it.

The dog that catches and runs off with the hare is the winner, but often the hare escapes. In such a situation, the formal judge awards points to determine the winning dog and the winning bettors. While the chase is in progress, he awards a point to the dog that forces the hare to change direction for the first time and again for the last time before the hare escapes. He will also award a point for a "go-by," when one dog passes the other on a straightaway.

The Wrong Side of the River

All major capital cities of Europe have a "wrong side of town," and London is no exception. However, it has a "wrong side of the river." Everyone knows about the goings-on in Southwark on the south bank of the Thames. Some visitors may find it attractive while others find it repugnant.

Southwark's reputation as a disreputable part of town stems from its location at the southern end of the bridge across the Thames, outside the walls of London. Southwark is a place of poverty for most and has no curfew and very few laws. This combination of conditions creates a dangerous and, for some, very exciting place to visit. The character of this area is driven by its alehouses, bordellos, theaters, and raucous entertainment houses.

Of the approximately 400 alehouses in all of London, 228 are in Southwark, which accounts for only 10 percent of London's population. Roughly, every fourth establishment is an alehouse, creating a considerable problem of drunkenness. Many in London believe that these alehouses threaten public order and remain a hotbed of promiscuity. Unfortunately, they flourish because London officials do not come to the area.

Accompanying the high number of public alehouses are the bordellos, commonly called "stews" by the locals. Thomas Nash visited Southwark in 1592 and is quoted in Leonard R.N. Ashley's book *Elizabethan Popular Culture:* "London, what are thy suburbs but licensed stews? Can it be so many brothel houses of salary sensuality and sixpence whoredome should be set up and maintained? Gentlemen's purses and pockets they [the women] will dive into and pick, even whiles they are dallying with them."

Many of the alehouses work in concert with bordellos in a clandestine manner. When the men become drunk, they are taken upstairs to a bordello; the next morning, they find themselves asleep on the street, without their money. King Henry VIII attempted to banish these ladies, without success, and Queen Elizabeth passed a law that forbade watermen from leading customers to the stews during hours of darkness.

Southwark is also London's entertainment zone. It is home to many theaters and to bear- and bull-baiting rings. Added to these permanent establishments are temporary tents for itinerant entertainers such as acrobats, ballad singers, clowns, fencers, and puppeteers. This area provides a virtually continuous performance of one sort or another every day of the year. Although some of this may seem harmless, it attracts many pickpockets, adding to the already high crime rate.

Bear baiting is a popular, although dangerous, spectacle. Here, an enraged bear refuses to confine himself to the ring.

Bear Baiting

Bear baiting is another sport popular in London. It takes place in the Bear Garden, which is a ring of covered seats surrounding a circular arena. Bear baiting consists of setting a pack of crazed hounds loose on a bear chained to a post and watching from a safe distance while the bear fends off the attacking hounds. This bloody spectacle, popular with the working classes, is occasionally attended by royalty.

The dogs rarely kill the bear, but they often bite it ferociously on the nose and neck, causing it to bleed profusely. One bear named Sackerson fought for so many years that it became a public favorite. As for the dogs, the loss of a leg usually kills most of them. And on occasion, a swipe by the bear's claw rips the poor animal open, sending it flying into the crowd. It is this sort of bloodletting that particularly excites the spectators.

Bear baiting was a favorite of the queen, who often invited friends to join her at the ring. One such friend, Robert Laneham, watched the sport and provided this account of what he saw:

It was a sport very pleasant to see the bear with his pink eyes leering after his enemies' approach, the nimbleness and wait of the dogs to take his advantage, and the force and experience of the bear to avoid the assaults. If he were bitten in one place, how he would pinch in another to get free: that if he were taken once, then what shift, with biting, with clawing, with roaring, tossing and tumbling he would work to wind himself from them: and when he was loose, to shake his ears twice or thrice with the blood and the slaver [drool] about his face was a matter of goodly relief.[19]

The bear-baiting ring is located next to the bull-baiting ring, where the same sort of sport takes place but with bulls instead of bears.

Public Executions

For truly macabre entertainment, public executions occur quite frequently.

Public capital punishments are popular with the London working class. Executions are either beheadings or hangings depending on the offense, the person's social standing, and the whim of the judge.

The only way foreigners are likely to see a beheading is if one is taking place at the Tower. Although not all beheadings at the Tower are public, many are, and they are well attended. Scaffolding is erected around the site and the chopping block is set on the ground. The prisoner is brought out to the cheers of the crowd and is offered the opportunity to speak. Some say a few words, while others remain silent. Both the wives of King Henry VIII, for example, spoke briefly in Latin, asking God to receive their souls. An eyewitness to the execution of the earl of Essex in 1601 recorded his last moments:

The Earl suffered on Ash Wednesday within the Tower of London between 7 and 8 in the morning. He was brought out by a lieutenant who attended on him, and three guards. All the way to the scaffold he prayed, saying "O Lord, give me true repentance, and true patience, and true humility." Then he turned to the noblemen who sat on the scaffolding and put off his hat and confessed all his crimes. Then he called for the executioner. Then he asked the executioner what he must do and how

Public execution by hanging or decapitation is a decidedly ghoulish, but quite common, source of diversion in London.

he must lie. Then he knelt down and laid his neck on the block . . . and spreading his arms wide and stretching his body out he prayed to Jesus. And so with three strokes the executioner struck off his head, and when the head was off and in the executioner's hand, the eyes did open and shut.[20]

The executioner stands ready with either an ax that he swings around, over his head, and then down upon the person's neck, or a two-handed sword that is raised above his head and then brought straight down on the neck. The two-handed sword is preferred by all condemned persons because it is more accurate and the executioner is less likely to accidentally strike the person's shoulders or back before hitting the neck.

Tourists are more likely to witness a hanging. Most take place at gallows just outside the city wall, but occasionally hangings occur at the scene of the crime. Hangings are particularly

The Pillory: Law and Order in London

Although it is not a formal type of entertainment, Londoners love wandering down a street and finding young men (and occasionally ladies) locked in a pubic pillory for some crime they committed. A pillory is a wood apparatus that clamps around a person's neck and hands, preventing the person from escaping. Without a formal police force to arrest and punish criminals, it becomes the job of responsible citizens to do so. When, for example, pickpockets, thieves, or prostitutes are caught by the citizenry, they are clamped in a pillory for the remainder of the day as their punishment. Londoners enjoy the sight because they know that justice is being served.

The pillory is a public place of discomfort and humiliation. Many of them can be found throughout London. Since the offenders cannot escape and their faces are exposed, passersby enjoy taunting them with verbal insults and sometimes pelting them with mud, animal feces, small stones, and dead fish. Occasionally as criminals stand in a pillory unable to protect themselves, some lose their sight when hit in the eyes with small stones; others are whipped from behind.

Not all criminals are released at the end of the day unscarred by the experience. On occasion, criminals are nailed to a pillory with a nail driven through one ear. At the end of the day, the person's head is released either by removing the nail with a pair of pliers or by tearing the ear from the nail with a quick pull on the head.

popular and exciting because the prisoners, often several packed into a cart, are pulled down Holborn and Oxford Streets followed by anyone who can spare the time to witness the execution. Crowds are large and are usually made up of as many women as men. All the way to the gallows, the condemned are jeered by the crowd, who are hoping to see panic written on their faces or, even better, a futile attempt at escape.

Once the condemned arrive at the gallows, the noose is placed around each neck and each is given a brief opportunity to speak. Such an opportunity is generally a mistake because the crowd heckles and ridicules whatever is said. When the speeches are over, the executioner pushes the prisoner off the scaffold and the crowd cheers with each twist and kick until the victim dies.

Occasionally, the punishment stipulates that the condemned is to be "drawn and quartered," meaning that the person is hanged but cut down before he is dead. Then, in a state of semiconsciousness, his belly is drawn open with a sword and disemboweled and the body cut into four parts. William Harrison, who witnessed this punishment, reported,

> They are hanged till they be half dead and then taken down and quartered alive; after that their members and bowels are cut from their bodies and thrown into a fire provided near-hand and within their own sight.[21]

Sometimes, instead of burning the body parts, they are hung in different districts of the city as a deterrent to crime. However, hooligans in the crowd, often teenage boys, sometimes run off with the parts first.

Although London can provide many types of entertainment, from theater to executions, many other nearby towns and cities have their own distinctive attractions worth exploring. For those with time, many interesting smaller towns offer visitors sights and experiences that cannot be found in the more noisy, more expensive, and often more crowded city of London. For both rural beauty and historic importance, the cities of Canterbury, Oxford, the Isle of Wight, and Portsmouth are recommended.

CHAPTER EIGHT

Around and About London

Canterbury

Sixty miles southeast of London lies the city of Canterbury, England's most revered religious attraction. Canterbury is the home of the Church of England and home to Canterbury Cathedral, which was constructed between 1070 and 1180. Every year, thousands of pilgrims from all over England make the trek here to visit this sacred shrine where Archbishop Thomas à Becket was murdered by four of King Henry's soldiers in 1170.

The Canterbury Cathedral, which is the main attraction of the city, stands within the city's walls. Enter through the great Christ Church Gate and proceed directly to the cathedral. Of particular note as points of interest are the crypt with intriguing carvings atop the columns, wall paintings from the 1200s, and the tomb of the Black Prince, a warrior known at the time as the "hero of the English people," which includes a display of his breastplate and sword. The most worshiped site, however, is the spot where Archbishop Becket knelt at the time he was struck in the neck and then the head by a sword. There is now a white square of marble marking the very spot where Becket's head hit the floor.

Canterbury is an important part of England's literary tradition as well. *The Canterbury Tales*, written by Geoffrey Chaucer two hundred years ago, tells a series of stories about a group of people who are making a pilgrimage, or holy trip, from London to the shrine of St. Thomas à Becket. Chaucer got the idea for the stories when he himself went on a pilgrimage and noticed the many fascinating people in the group.

Queen Elizabeth visited the city several times, even celebrating her fortieth birthday here in 1573. On another occasion she traveled to Canterbury to interview the Duc d'Alencon with a view to marriage. She is said to have met him in what is now the Queen Elizabeth Tea Rooms in the High Street, which can be enjoyed today by visitors.

Oxford

Sixty-five miles northwest of London is the city of Oxford on the Thames River. Founded during the tenth and eleventh centuries as an early Saxon trading settlement at the confluence of the Thames and Cherwell Rivers,

A view of Canterbury Cathedral. Many travelers make the pilgrimage from London to Canterbury to stand before the holy spot where Archbishop Thomas à Becket was martyred.

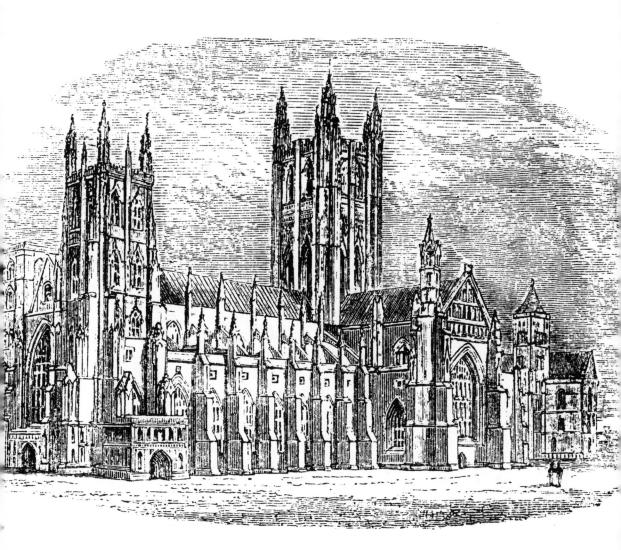

Oxford took its name from a narrow spot where oxen forded the river. Today, the city is famous throughout England and Europe as the home of one of the finest universities.

There is no clear founding date for Oxford University, but teaching existed at Oxford in some form in 1096 and developed rapidly after 1167, when King Henry II banned English students

Thomas à Becket

Thomas à Becket was born nearly five hundred years ago in London to a well-to-do family of merchants. His family money allowed him to receive an excellent education, first in London and later in Paris. When Becket was twenty-five, he took a job working for his uncle, the archbishop of Canterbury, Theobald of Bec.

In 1161, when Bec died, King Henry II appointed Becket the archbishop of Canterbury. Although the two enjoyed an amiable relationship initially, in 1164 the king issued sixteen edicts that restricted the authority of the church in legal matters and clearly stated that the authority of the king was greater than the authority of the archbishop.

Becket refused to accept the edicts. After a bitter six-year dispute while exiled in France, Becket returned to Canterbury in 1170 to reconcile with Henry. Rather than reconciliation, however, Becket infuriated the king with a sermon criticizing him. Frustrated after a decade of unhappiness with his choice of Becket as archbishop, Henry allegedly uttered the fatal question "Who will rid me of this turbulent priest?"

In response to the king's question, four of his knights rode to Canterbury on December 29. Following a heated argument, the knights struggled to drag Becket from the cathedral—because to kill him there would have been a supreme act of sacrilege. Becket, however, would not budge. While Becket knelt in prayer, believing the knights would not dare harm him in God's church, one of the knights drew his sword and ran it through his neck while another sliced off the top of his skull.

Becket's murder remains the best known and most shocking act in English history during the past 450 years. After the murder, pilgrims by the thousands began visiting the place of his death, forcing Henry to walk on his knees to the altar as an act of penance. Today, many people still make the pilgrimage to Canterbury to see where Becket was martyred.

from attending the University of Paris. The first colleges began as medieval residence halls for students under the supervision of a master. The first three colleges, University, Merton, and Balliol, were formed in the thirteenth century. They were immediately perceived as providing educational opportunities for young men wishing to enter the clergy, law, finances, medicine, science, and the military. Since then, twelve additional colleges have been established.

Several of the colleges have walls for the protection of the students in case of civil strife, which occasionally flared between the university and the city. Often referred to as "gown and town" controversies because of the distinctive black gowns worn by students, rioting between the two groups was particularly severe during the thirteenth century. Today, however, there is no noticeable friction between the groups.

Visitors to Oxford today will be able to wander through any of the fifteen colleges that presently make up Oxford University. Each of the colleges has its own chapel, dormitory for the young men, dining hall for students and faculty (who are called dons), and beautifully manicured lawns and gardens. Equally enjoyable is renting a small boat, called a punt, and drifting on the calm waters of the Thames River, which is quite narrow at this point on its journey to the sea.

Before departing Oxford, a trip to three of the city's most notable landmarks is recommended. The first is the eleventh-century church of St. Michael, then the thirteenth-century church of St. Mary the Virgin, and finally the newly constructed Bodleian Library, the largest in England.

Isle of Wight

Southwest of London lies the Isle of Wight, just a short boat trip off the coast from the port city of Portsmouth. This small 380-square-mile island is a favorite among London's elite as a vacation place during the summer months because it is the warmest spot in all of England. Although the water is warm enough for bathing, the warm summer sun, the white sandy beaches, and the dramatic country scenery attract many tourists.

One of the great sites worth visiting while touring the island is Yarmouth Castle. This coastal fort is just one in a chain of defense works that runs from Milford Haven in the west to Hull in the east. Henry VIII built these defenses in response to the threat of invasion from France and Spain. The castle is open to tourists every day.

A second place to visit on the island is Carisbrooke Castle, an eighth-century Saxon fortification that towers over the Isle of Wight on an artificial hill in the center of the island. The castle has been enlarged over the past

Student Life at Oxford

Although students attending Oxford are largely from the privileged classes, student life is far from luxurious. Students live modestly, not opulently, in various college dormitories. Few of today's three thousand students can afford their own books because most are still handwritten on expensive parchment. Consequently, much that is learned is done so by rote memorization. Meals are also simple for most students, as is evidenced by a favorite dessert called "college pudding," the least expensive dessert on the menu, consisting of two-day-old bread, raisins, sugar, and milk.

When students enter the university today, it is assumed that they learned Latin grammar thoroughly at some primary or "grammar" school. These language skills are reinforced by lectures in Latin and by the requirement that boys speak Latin in all classes, during meals, and in dormitories.

Upon admission to the university, each boy is required to spend four years learning basic liberal arts and mastering the rules of logic. If he passes his examinations, he receives the preliminary degree of bachelor of arts, which confers little distinction. To assure himself a place in professional life, he then must devote additional years to the pursuit of an advanced degree, such as a master of arts or doctor of laws, medicine, or theology. Those pursuing a doctorate in theology are particularly dedicated because it requires twelve years after the roughly eight years taken for a master of arts.

Unfortunately, despite strict rules of conduct and the threat of corporeal punishment or imprisonment, problems exist among university boys. The problems range from illicit drinking, gambling, prostitution, poaching of animals, and brawls to an occasional full-scale riot that requires army intervention. Such student behavior makes for bad reputations among townspeople, who deeply resent the superior status of the students. Part of the problem stems from the immaturity of many new students who arrive between the ages of twelve and fifteen.

Despite the appearance of equal treatment for all students, academic standards are occasionally relaxed for noble students in order to secure gifts of money from their fathers. Such occasionally uneven treatment is not surprising to the other students, who must find benefactors willing to pay for their university education.

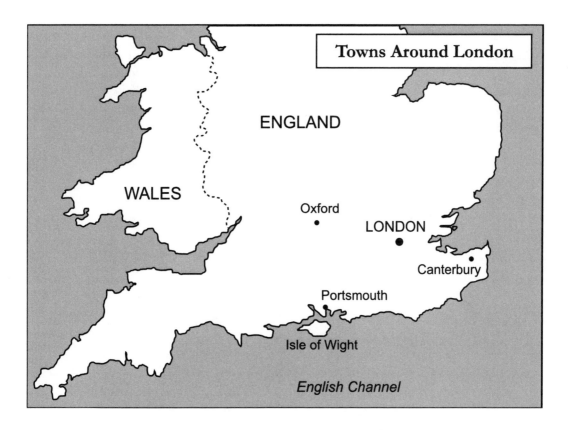

eight hundred years. The resulting architecture represents every phase of early English history from Saxon times to the present.

Portsmouth

The port city of Portsmouth, seventy miles southwest of London, is England's most famous and most active naval port. King Richard I founded the city in 1194 on the site of a Roman camp dating to the second century A.D. For tourists interested in English naval history, this is the place to walk the docks and visit several warships. For visitors interested in Roman history, there are also several Roman attractions.

Because Portsmouth sits along a strip of coast across from the Isle of Wight, the inlet creates a natural port protected from the high seas. It was because of its location and its proximity to France that the king granted the city a charter to build the Royal Dockyard here in 1496. As the traditional home of the Royal Navy, many of the fleet's ships are moored in Portsmouth.

The favorite ship for visitors to see is Henry VIII's flagship *Mary Rose*. Built between 1509 and 1511, the *Mary Rose* is a four-masted frigate and was the first English warship capable of firing a fifteen-cannon broadside on either side of the ship. In addition to the *Mary Rose*, many of the ships that fought and defeated the Spanish Armada in 1588 can still be seen.

A short walk north leads to the castle of Porchester, built next to a Roman defensive wall and the foundations of several buildings. The Romans defended this piece of land fearing a possible invasion by Gallic tribes across the Channel in France. Of interest are the ways the stones used here were cut and held together with cement, its earliest use in England.

Notes

Introduction: The Elizabethan Age

1. John Stow, *Survey of London*, ed. Henry Morley. London: George Routledge and Sons, 1893, p. 22.

Chapter 2: Weather and Location

2. Quoted in Leonard R.N. Ashley, *Elizabethan Popular Culture*. Bowling Green, OH: Bowling Green State University Press, 1988, p. 6.

3. Quoted in Maureen Waller, *1700: Scenes from London Life*. New York: Four Walls Eight Windows, 2000, p. 227.

4. Quoted in A.L. Rowse, *The Elizabethan Age: The England of Elizabeth: The Structure of Society*. New York: Macmillan, 1962, p. 214.

Chapter 3: Arriving in London, Where to Stay, and Where to Eat

5. William Harrison, *The Description of England*, ed. George Edelen. Ithaca, NY: Cornell University Press, 1968, p. 397.

6. Quoted in Steven Earnshaw, "The Altered State: England, Literature, and the Pub." www.shu.ac.uk.

7. Quoted in Waller, *1700*, p. 177.

8. Quoted in M. St. Claire Bryne, *Elizabethan Life in Town and Country*. London: Methuen, 1961, p. 61.

Chapter 4: Historical Monuments of London

9. Quoted in "The History of the Tower of London," Historic Royal Palaces. www.hrp.org.uk.

10. Quoted in *"Westminster Abbey Tour: Edward the Confessor's Chapel."* www.westminster-abbey.org.

Chapter 5: Casual Sightseeing

11. Quoted in Ashley, *Elizabethan Popular Culture*, p. 5.

Chapter 6: Shopping

12. Quoted in Waller, *1700*, p. 1.

13. Quoted in Waller, *1700*, p. 172.

14. Quoted in Ashley, *Elizabethan Popular Culture*, p. 8.

15. Quoted in Waller, *1700*, p. 156.

16. Quoted in Drea Leed, "Sumptuary Laws in Tudor England: Is Your Garb Legal?" Elizabethan Costuming Page. www.dnaco.net.

Chapter 7: Entertainment

17. Quoted in "Renaissance Art and Architecture," Emory University. www.emory.edu.

18. Quoted in Ashley, *Elizabethan Popular Culture*, p. 5.

19. Quoted in Ashley, *Elizabethan Popular Culture*, p. 175.

20. Quoted in David Birt, *Elizabeth's England*. London: Longman Group, 1981, pp. 12–13.

21. Harrison, *The Description of England*, p. 187.

For Further Reading

A.L. Beier and Roger Finlay, *London 1500-1700: The Making of the Metropolis*. London: Longman, 1986. This book is an excellent history of London during the Renaissance that manages to capture the growth of the city during the period of the Tudors and the Stuarts. Emphasis is placed on private estates and municipal buildings.

Stephen Humphrey, *Churches and Cathedrals of London*. London: New Holland Press, 2000. This work presents a visually stunning picture of London's religious architecture. Each era in London's long and complex history is documented, including Romanesque, Gothic, Baroque, and Neoclassical. The book explores the art, architecture, history, and legend associated with nearly fifty of London's best-known churches and cathedrals.

Edward Impey and Geoffrey Parnell, *The Tower of London: The Official Illustrated History*. London: Merrell, in association with Historic Royal Palaces, 2000. This book is written in two parts. The first part covers the Tower during the Middle Ages, which is largely architectural information about the start and development of the castles. The second part continues telling the story of the physical history of the Tower, but talks more about its functions and role in the history of England.

Francis Sheppard, *London: A History*. Oxford, England: Oxford University Press, 1998. This comprehensive history of London offers a clearly written and concise overview of London's history, from its founding by the Romans to the present. Sheppard takes the reader from the Romans through plagues, fires, rebellions, and riots in a lucid chronological narrative. He also provides descriptions of tavern life, theatrical events, and an endless supply of royal intrigue.

Works Consulted

Books

Leonard R.N. Ashley, *Elizabethan Popular Culture*. Bowling Green, OH: Bowling Green State University Press, 1988. This book is a compilation of primary-source documentation from the Elizabethan age. Its focus is on the sociology of the time, with descriptions of people's lives as they move about London and its many public gathering places.

David Birt, *Elizabeth's England*. London: Longman Group, 1981. Birt's book records events occurring between 1509 and 1603. It focuses on the Tower of London, palaces of London, ministers of Queen Elizabeth, English universities, and London's alehouses and inns. The book integrates primary sources with contemporary observations.

M. St. Claire Bryne, *Elizabethan Life in Town and Country*. London: Methuen, 1961. A scholarly book on the social lives and activities of the English during the time of Queen Elizabeth. The book touches on all classes, rich and poor, and provides a lively dialogue that includes quotations from many notable writers of the period.

William Harrison, *The Description of England*. Ed. George Edelen. Ithaca, NY: Cornell University Press, 1968. During the mid-1500s, William Harrison journeyed extensively through England noting how people were living their lives. The result of his observations is this important work providing insight into such topics as food and diet, laws, clothing, punishments for criminals, castles and palaces, dogs, fish, cattle, languages, and dozens of other topics describing everyday life in England.

Jo McMurtry, *Understanding Shakespeare's England: A Companion for the American Reader*. Hamdon, CT: Anchor Books, 1989. This work captures the spirit of England and London during the Tudor period. The author focuses on the history, social classes, customs, and everyday experiences of the people.

A.L. Rowse, *The Elizabethan Age: The England of Elizabeth: The Structure of Society*. New York: Macmillan, 1962. This book focuses on the structure of Elizabethan society in terms of its historical achievements. It is organized into twelve chapters, each of which addresses a major social organization such as the cities, the church, the social classes, and the law.

Jeffrey L. Singman, *Daily Life in Elizabethan England*. Westport, CT: Greenwood Press, 1995. Singman provides a lively description of life in sixteenth-century England that includes such things as food recipes, details about clothing, games, popular songs, and everyday activities for the noble and commoners alike.

Lawrence Stone, *Crisis of the Aristocracy*. Oxford, England: Oxford University Press, 1967. This book examines the decline of the court-centered aristocracy in England during the early periods following William the Conqueror and its rise to power and prestige under the Tudors. It also traces the life of the various classes of noblemen, such as lords, barons, earls, counts, and dukes and their relationship with the Crown, with particular reference to the reign of Queen Elizabeth.

John Stow, *Survey of London*. Ed. Henry Morley. London: George Routledge and Sons, 1893. John Stow wrote a series of chronicles between 1565 and 1604 that describe many people, places, and activities in London during the reign of Queen Elizabeth. This edited book captures the spirit of the chronicles while providing wonderful insights into London life.

Simon Thurley, *Royal Palaces of Tudor England*. New Haven, CT: Yale University Press, 1993. This beautifully illustrated book describes in detail the royal palaces of the Tudor period, including Hampton Court Palace, the Tower of London, Greenwich Palace, St. James' Palace, Nonesuch, Whitehall, and Richmond Palace, as well as several minor palaces. Each palace is discussed in terms of architecture and court life.

Maureen Waller, *1700: Scenes from London Life*. New York: Four Walls Eight Windows, 2000. This work contains primary-source material as well as sociological observation about London during the 1700s, although the material overlaps this period. The book is arranged into sixteen chapters, each representing a different social institution.

Edward Wessex, *Crown and Country: A Personal Guide to Royal London*. New York: Universe, 2001. This book is by Prince Edward, who writes a short history and provides beautiful color photographs of dozens of landmarks in London and the city's environs.

Periodicals

"A Book of Orders and Rules," edited from the original manuscript by Sir Sibbald David Scott, *Sussex Archaeological Collections*, vol. 7, 1854.

Websites

The Altered State: England, Literature, and the Pub (www.shu.ac.uk). Steven Earnshaw created this website containing sixteenth-century quotations from English writers describing inns, taverns, and pubs of the time.

Britannia (www.britannia.com). This site provides a complete and detailed history of London from prehistoric times to the present.

Chaucer: The Canterbury Tales (www.siue.edu). This is an electronic version of Chaucer's *Canterbury Tales* both in old English and in modern English.

Elizabethan Costuming Page (www.dnaco.net). This website provides detailed descriptions and pictures of men's and women's clothing during sixteenth-century England.

Emory University (www.emory.edu). This is the website for the entire university. It contains links to all departments and all research carried out under the auspices of the university.

His Majestie King James I & VI Page (www.jesus-is-lord.com). This website focuses exclusively on King James, his work, his personal writings, the literature of his time, and society during his reign.

Historic Royal Palaces (www.hrp.org.uk). This website presents photos and histories of five royal palaces in London, providing architectural history, social history, and a variety of little known facts that bring each palace to life.

River Thames Guide (www.riverthames.co.uk). This website is a guide to the Thames River and the areas through which it flows. The site offers a history of the river, how it was perceived during the Elizabethan era, and the many attractions along its banks.

University of Virginia Library Electronic Text Center (http:// etext.lib.virginia.edu). This website offers a large number of electronic, historical, and literary works.

Westminster Abbey: Place of Worship, House of Kings (www.westminster-abbey.org). This website provides a history of the abbey, discussions of its architecture, events that continue to take place, and answers to frequently asked questions.

Index

Picture Credits

Cover © Art Resource, NY

Guildhall Art Gallery, Corporation of London,UK/Bridgeman Art Library, 26

Private Collection/ Bridgeman Art Library, 72, 85

Victoria and Albert Museum/ Bridgeman Art Library, 49

© Bettmann/CORBIS, 14

© Historical picture Archive/CORBIS, 54, 58, 62

© Martin Jones/CORBIS, 56

© Gianni Dagli Orti/CORBIS, 16

© the Mariner's museum/CORBIS, 77

© Lenard de Silva/ CORBIS, 53

Krishna Cokal, 24, 52, 97

Chris Jouan, 66, 81

Library of Congress, 11

Mary Evans Picture Library, 29, 64, 74–75

North Wind Picture Archives, 12, 17, 18, 20, 35, 37, 38, 41, 47, 55, 57, 59, 63, 71, 76, 83, 93

Stock Montage, Inc. 27, 40, 44, 67, 70, 82, 87, 89

About the Author

James Barter received his undergraduate degree in history and classics at the University of California, Berkeley, followed by graduate studies in ancient history and archaeology at the University of Pennsylvania. Mr. Barter has taught history as well as Latin and Greek.

A Fulbright scholar at the American Academy in Rome, Mr. Barter worked on archaeological sites in and around the city as well as on sites in the Naples area. Mr. Barter also has worked and traveled extensively in Greece.

Mr. Barter currently lives in Rancho Santa Fe, California, with his seventeen-year-old daughter, Kalista. Mr. Barter's older daughter, Tiffany Modell, also lives in Rancho Santa Fe.

DATE DUE

12-1-04			

FOLLETT